"In *Part-time Pastor, Full-time Church*, Bob LaRochelle gives small membership churches a necessary resource for their emerging ministry through theoretical reflection and practical suggestions. Small congregations looking for new visions of pastoral leadership will find in his book a theologically sound and thoughtful model to consider. His experience in bivocational ministry, his breadth of experience in Roman Catholic and Protestant churches, and his love for the small membership church give him a unique perspective on pastoral responsibilities and the needs of the church. *Part-time Pastor, Full-time Church* provides a much needed and helpful resource to congregations, pastoral search committees, and clergy looking for practical advice about how to establish a successful ministry with part-time pastoral leadership."

—THE REV. DR. RONALD B. BROWN,
Associate Conference Minister for Clergy Concerns,
Connecticut Conference, United Church of Christ

"The American religious landscape is changing, and the American clergy should change with it. Bob LaRochelle, long-time UCC pastor, has some ideas that could make all the difference for churches struggling to find a place in the new landscape, from how to stay connected when the pastor has a second job, to how to build community when there are so many tugs on everyone's time."

—SUSAN CAMPBELL,
columnist for the *Hartford Courant* (Connecticut) and author of *Dating Jesus*

"*Part-time Pastor, Full-time Church* is a timely and helpful contribution that explores fresh leadership perspectives and practices for smaller membership churches. This book offers wise, practical guidance to churches and clergy seeking to offer faithful and effective witness through bivocational models of ministry."

—W. DOW EDGERTON,
Professor of Ministry, Chicago Theological Seminary

"Like your day job, but also feel called to ministry? Perhaps you are a small congregation seeking a part-time pastor—or a growing church needing additional ministerial leadership? Or are you part of a denomination caught in demographic changes that is likely to need more bivocational pastors? Then read LaRochelle's insightful book. He knows of what he writes and acts as a guide into the growing world of multiple callings."

—RICH KIRCHHERR,
senior pastor, First Congregational Church, Western Springs, Illinois

"*Part-time Pastor, Full-time Church* serves as a ringing affirmation for valuing a church's ministry not by whether it has full-time or part-time pastoral leadership, the number of Sunday worshipers, nor the size of the budget; but by the depth of its faithfulness and the vitality of its congregational life. LaRochelle also offers proven suggestions to manage time, communication, and technology to balance the needs of congregation, secular job, and family. Any pastor or church considering part-time ministry will find no better resource for entering into a fruitful relationship with eyes wide open."

—REV. DOUGLAS STIVISON,
pastor, First Congregational UCC, Haworth, New Jersey, and
former editor and publisher of *The Living Pulpit*

"Bob LaRochelle faces squarely and without anxiety the realities that surround many mainline churches today as they look to the possibility of moving towards part-time ministry. He offers a straight-on analysis and suggestions for how a church can move into a healthy, vital new chapter with eyes wide open and with hope for the future. Additionally, the reader gets a glimpse of a real-life scenario that 'works,' played out every Sunday in rural Connecticut. Each section contains guidance for a church community exploring the possibility of a part-time or bivocational minister. LaRochelle has considered each step carefully and walks the reader through the many questions that come up at every turn. This book should be a primary resource for church leadership entering into this stage of discernment."

—THE REV. DR. PAUL TELLSTRÖM,
senior pastor, Irvine United Congregational Church, United Church of Christ

Part-time Pastor, Full-time Church

Robert LaRochelle

THE PILGRIM PRESS
CLEVELAND

D e d i c a t i o n

*To my wife, Tricia,
who has inspired me
and supported me as
I have journeyed on
this bivocational road,
with gratitude that
our marriage is the
most important of all
the vocations that I
will ever have!*

The Pilgrim Press, 700 Prospect Avenue, Cleveland, Ohio 44115
thepilgrimpress.com
© 2010 by Robert LaRochelle

Printed in the United States of America on acid-free paper

14   13   12   11   5   4   3

Library of Congress Cataloging-in-Publication Data

LaRochelle, Robert, 1953–
      Part-time pastor, full-time church / Robert LaRochelle.
      p. cm.
  Includes bibliographical references (p.   ).
  ISBN 978-0-8298-1871-0 (alk. paper)
  1. Clergy, Part-time. I. Title.
BV676.5.L37 2010
253'.2—dc22   2010033706

CONTENTS

Acknowledgments

Many people contributed to the ongoing formulation of ideas that led to the development of this book. In particular, I wish to thank the congregation of the Congregational Church of Union, Connecticut, UCC, for the opportunity to serve alongside them, for their ongoing support, and for their willingness to engage both faithfully and creatively in the work of being a small mainstream church that is wonderfully progressive, alive, and willing to respond to twenty-first century needs.

I thank Timothy Staveteig, former publisher at The Pilgrim Press, for his constructive feedback as I sought to develop a text that would address a real need in the contemporary church and be useful to those who would seek to read it. I thank Kim Martin Sadler, editorial director at The Pilgrim Press, for her guidance, insights, and suggestions, and my students and colleagues in the South Windsor (Connecticut) Public Schools, among whom I have shared an important vocation in my life. In particular, I thank my dear friends in our school's Counseling Department. Special thanks also to Kristin Firth, copyeditor for this project, who was so helpful and thorough in guiding me through this, my first book.

I wish to thank our children: Brian, who has just begun a career as a school counselor and baseball coach; Kathleen, entering her third year at Yale Divinity School; and our youngest, Stephen, embarking on his first year at Hamilton College this fall, for all of their input and good humor and for putting up with listening to my many opinions on a wide array of topics over the years. To the three of you and to your mom, Patricia, with whom I have shared thirty wonderful years: Thanks, and I love you deeply and forever!

Introduction

Over the past several years, both formal studies and anecdotal evidence have indicated that the American religious
landscape is changing. The most recent study released by
Trinity College in 2009 makes quite clear what we have known for
awhile.[1] The evidence in this report indicates that there has been
significant growth in the so called "evangelical"[2] forms of Protestant Christianity, including the many megachurches that have
arisen throughout this country. Concurrently, there has been a significant decline in what has been called traditional "mainline
Protestant Christianity" including such long-established and well-
known denominations as the Episcopal Church, the United
Church of Christ, the United Methodist Church, and many others.
In many local communities, interdenominational, "Bible-based"

churches have been quite successful in marking significant growth while their mainline counterparts clearly struggle to retain their congregational vitality or even their existence.

This decline in the mainline church is a phenomenon found in cities, suburbs, and small towns alike. Urban congregations face major losses in membership due to demographic trends involving both a pattern of considerable movement to suburbia and the aging population of their congregations. Within urban areas, a proliferation of storefront and evangelical churches has shown success in drawing new church members. In both suburbs and small towns, denominational identification has been weakened and churches increasingly find themselves losing both potential as well as current members to those churches that offer a multiplicity of programs for people of all ages.

It goes without saying that these very real changes have created financial burdens for mainline churches. Even prior to the well-publicized economic crisis that came burgeoning onto the American scene at the end of 2008, these churches were feeling the effect of this involuntary downsizing that has been several years in the making. As a result, local churches have struggled to make ends meet, provide valuable programs for varied constituencies within their congregation, and pay the kind of salary that might draw quality pastoral leadership. Churches that would like to offer programs that could draw youth the way those churches down the road are able to do find themselves incapable financially of hiring the youth director or director of Christian education whom they need. On an annual basis, as each budgetary cycle unfolds, they are faced with making tough, often unpalatable choices in order to sustain what they have, frequently causing within them increased consternation that because of these choices they simply cannot grow or expand, much less provide the kind of mainstream alternative to "evangelical" Christianity they are convinced the church of Jesus Christ really needs.

The premise of this book is that, as a result of these well-documented demographic and financial shifts and in fidelity to the mission of the mainline church and the denominations in which these churches exist, it is incumbent upon these communities of faith to evaluate new ways of providing pastoral leadership. This reevaluation includes an openness to the possibility of calling a part-time or bivocational pastor to tend to the needs of their congregations. Of equal importance, however, is the accompanying premise that a church can "downsize" to a part-time pastor while retaining and maybe even developing its identity as a thriving, vital full-time church!

There are those who will read this book who might be threatened by this notion. There are church councils and search committees who would be deeply troubled by the suggestion that they consider restructuring so as to consider part-time pastoral service. They would argue that in doing so, their church in effect becomes less than it has always been. It is important as I lay out this blueprint for possible reevaluation that I, at the same time, affirm the clear validity of their concern. First and foremost must be the clear recognition that in any church of any size or model of pastoral leadership, certain realities have to exist:

- It is important that good preaching and worship occur.

- It is important that individuals, including shut-ins and hospitalized persons, receive good pastoral care.

- It is important that the pastor be available to members of his or her congregation for advice, counsel, direction, and overall leadership.

- It is important that the pastor be an important voice on those boards and committees within the church in which the pastor's presence and participation is required.

- It is important that the pastor engage in ongoing, consistent dialogue and collaboration with other members of the church staff.

- Overall, it is important that the pastor is able to respond well to the needs of the pastoral role as developed responsibly within each congregation.

I contend that it is very possible—with creative thinking and restructuring on the part of the church and with necessary skills on the part of the pastor—for part-time and bivocational pastors to serve churches well. In this book I attempt to lay out specific, practical ways for that to occur. In doing so, I do not attempt to either downplay or denigrate the importance and work of the full-time pastor; rather, I would argue that it is in the best interest of a very large number of churches to have at least one full-time ordained leader on staff. But many churches might benefit from an openness to restructuring. For those that do, there are effective ways that pastors can serve in this part-time capacity, whereby a church will find it is receiving the kind of quality pastoral service it both needs and deserves.

To develop this point, I begin in our first chapter by exploring in detail the changing pastoral realities of life in the modern church. I contrast church life "as it was" and how it is in the ideal church of our memories and imaginations with the realities of church life within the contemporary context. In chapter 2, I look at the dynamics inherent in a congregation's process of reinterpreting itself and considering a reinterpretation of the pastoral role. This includes an honest examination of some of the negative self-perceptions underlying even the mere thought of evaluation and potential reinterpretation.

Since bivocational ministry is part of a strategy some churches consider, in chapter 3 I speak from my own personal experience to take a close look at both the possibilities and the pitfalls inherent in a bivocational, part-time model of pastoral leadership. In chapter 4, we look at a model of bivocational ministry that has been developed within the Roman Catholic Church and operative for over thirty years, the ordained ministry of permanent deacon. In doing so, we will be conscious of the distinctions between the deacon in Roman Catholic polity and the mainline Protestant model of pastor, yet make what will be for many some surprising comparisons reinforcing the claim that we can learn much from this approach to ordained ministry.

In the final three chapters, I attempt to be very specific and practical. In chapter 5, I spell out particular issues related to small churches, and in chapter 6, I make suggestions for search committees and candidates engaged in the process of considering a bivocational model and becoming a bivocational pastor within a local church. In chapter 7, I offer some conclusions regarding successful part-time and bivocational ministry, conclusions that I hope will lead to ongoing discussion in local churches, in seminaries, and within the leadership of America's mainline denominations.

I would be remiss in writing were I not to give you a brief glimpse at my background. I am currently serving in my tenth year as part-time pastor of the Congregational Church of Union, Connecticut, United Church of Christ. I am employed full-time as a counselor at a Connecticut public high school, where I have most recently served as varsity head baseball coach for several seasons, at times almost feeling trivocational! Prior to ordination in the UCC, I served as a Roman Catholic permanent deacon for nine years. During that time, I worked as both a public school employee and a paid staff member (youth minister, director of religious education) in Catholic parishes. As is probably obvious at this point, I hold the firm conviction that bivocational ministry is doable and that well-done, part-time ministry will not detract from and may in fact contribute toward the work of ministry in what is always a full-time church!

1

Changing Pastoral Realities

Once upon a time, in the heyday of mainline American Protestantism, the work of a pastor was fairly clear-cut. He or she (usually he!) would emerge from the church-owned parsonage and, with the exception of the traditional Monday and Saturday days off (barring weddings, funerals, and emergencies, of course), the pastor would go to his church office, also known as "the pastor's study," where he might spend several hours engaged in a variety of "pastoral" work. It was certainly not unusual for him to spend several hours a week in his office providing pastoral counseling and advice to members of the congregation. Back in the day, this pastor could count on a steady stream of appointments and phone calls from congregants. He might lead a morning or mid-week Bible study or attend a breakfast with organized groups in his congregation before attending to his other daily pastoral duties.

Depending upon the nature of the community in which the pastor was serving, there might even be some civic interaction during the day, luncheons with the Rotary Club or other civic organization, sometimes as leader of prayer or simply as trusted colleague and community pillar, involvement on committees with other full-time pastors and leaders of other faith communities, and various and sundry other duties and responsibilities that would keep him quite busy. In addition to all of this, it was expected that the pastor would maintain a steady schedule of visitation to nursing homes, hospitals, and the homebound and also make simple home visits to members of the congregation just to stay in touch.

The pastor's office (the study) was that place where each and every week he would spend countless hours studying scripture, researching material for and writing his sermon, and then working cooperatively with the secretary and music director to produce the important weekly worship bulletin for congregational use on Sundays. Depending upon the size of the congregation, the pastor could count on several standing meetings each month and an array of church events—suppers, luncheons, strawberry festivals, roast beef and pork dinners, and the like as well as such local events as Memorial Day parades and Fourth of July celebrations—at which his presence was deemed to be nonnegotiably necessary!

Well, I am here to argue that in this twenty-first century things have changed radically, and I am also convinced that there really is no turning back. It has been clear for several years that there just are not as many church people around during the day to visit the pastor as there used to be. For quite a few decades now, more and more women, for example, have been working outside of the home, and most people with children will tell you that with the proliferation of extracurricular possibilities for their children, family life is busier than ever. Even those individuals who serve actively on church boards and committees often make it quite clear that they don't really have that much time for church work, stretched as they are by all of the demands of modern life.

The end result of all of this, dare I say, is that parishioners just are not going to be stopping by the pastor's office as frequently as they used to. The modern pastor is discovering that the preponderance of church business and contact takes place during "nontraditional" hours. In other words, the real work of church business takes place at those weeknight meetings, and structuring Sunday mornings well can provide maximum possibility for both faith formation and governance activity within local churches. More than ever, emphasis now must be placed upon good planning in church programming, planning that is well thought out and conversant with the competing responsibilities with which the members of congregations must deal.

Yet there is more that is going on here. Once upon a time, more people sought to deal with family issues and even crippling emotional problems by seeking the counsel of their clergy. While many still do, it is quite clear that within mainline Christianity when people want to work on marriage problems, they are more inclined to book appointments with a marriage and family therapist than with their local minister. If they are down and depressed, it's not the pastor who will provide the Prozac, Zoloft, or ongoing psychotherapy they need. It's the mental health professional: the psychiatrist, clinical social worker, psychologist, or other certified therapist. It's not the pastor unless that pastor also has great credentials and specific training in one of those mental health fields, the kind of credentials not generally garnered in a generalized program of seminary study.

Truth be told, the pastor does not even need to go anywhere near his or her (another difference from decades ago is that many women are pastors today) office nowadays to do the biblical study needed to write her or his sermons. Sometimes the home office or Starbucks corner with laptop on a table can be a much better place to work. Much of the top line biblical and theological commentary and the entirety of the Bible itself, in its varied versions and translations, is available online.[1] In addition, assuming the pastor has a computer and a phone, the pastor and administrative assistant can coordinate that important weekly bulletin by phone and through cyberspace. Necessary conversations can be had with the music director that way as well.

In writing this, I am well aware that there are many who would quarrel not only with my analysis but also with its implications. Their objections simply must be taken very, very seriously. If a church has a full-time pastor who also has another job and/or is part-time, there are certain things that pastor cannot do. One could argue, for example, that such a pastor cannot be flexible enough to respond to a crisis and just be present at someone's side in an emergency, that fewer people will have the benefit of pastoral visitation, and that those who are isolated from the church because of illness or disability will feel even more isolated.

In addition, since clergy study groups and denominational conferences and committee meetings tend to occur during traditional daytime hours, a part-time pastor is less likely to reap the benefits from those activities and the congregation may lose out on something because that pastor is less involved than other churches' pastors. As an example, I have felt limited by my inability to attend clergy biblical study or to participate in my local association's committee on ministry because I work another full-time job. A pastor might be limited in forming necessary alliances to advocate for change and social justice and to engage in certain actions on behalf of important issues because he or she is simply not around during the day.

The bottom line is clear: Those who would argue against part-time or bivocational ministry tend to worry that their church would not receive the quality service it needs were this kind of approach to be embraced and adapted. They quite rightfully would assert that there is much necessary work for a pastor to do in a congregation and that it is important for a congregation to know a pastor is present. This argument and perspective cannot be overlooked and taken lightly.

Many clergy who might be very happy in their local congregations nonetheless have, at times, been willing to explore other possibilities available in other churches—possibilities often presented them by those denominational leaders who assist churches in their process of calling pastors. I, for one, have certainly done so, not out of eagerness to leave my congregation, but rather because I've been willing to look at how my skills might meet the needs of another congregation. I mention this in the context of this discussion about the issue of a pastor's physical presence.

One search committee with whom I was once actively engaged was willing to explore a part-time pastor after years of having nothing but full-time clergy. This willingness was coupled with reluctance among many congregants and, in my estimation, a deep-down fear that in going part-time, they would be losing something from their ordained leader. One of our discussions centered on their concern that in the bivocational model I was presenting, I would not be present the way they would want me to be. I countered that in my current congregation, I am most accessible and people can easily find me and speak with me. Yet, their concern that I was proposing not to be on the property as much as previous pastors was a very real one. My counter—that a "weekday" pastor doesn't necessarily have parishioners to be around with or for, and that I really didn't think people were going to come flocking to me for pastoral counseling during posted office hours—didn't exactly fly well with them. I ended up dropping out of the search process even as I sensed that they were leaning toward rolling the dice and taking a chance on me because I felt that I'd end up spending a lot of time battling the perception that I was not really present for them, a perception that has never been part of my ministry in my current congregation. I felt that I would be starting off a new call by fighting an uphill battle and I deemed that this could lead to a less than desirable relationship over the long haul.

It is quite understandable how a search committee, representing the intent of the congregation, might be afraid that the church they love would receive diminished service from a part-time pastor. Yet I must counter that this perception can be overcome if a congregation is willing to engage in a serious effort both to reinterpret what is needed from their pastor within their contemporary context and to look at what it means for a congregation as a whole to be engaged in the work of ministry.

This process of reinterpretation is one we shall explore in depth in the next chapter. Here I offer what I hope is a useful observation. Protestant Christians should really be in the forefront of those within the Christian tradition who are willing to explore new options. One of the driving principles of the Reformation that is as applicable to the twenty-first century as it was to the sixteenth is the notion of a church always ready and willing to reform its very self. As a result of the Reformation, modern Christianity has seen significant variety in the ways churches have organized themselves and their leadership. Experimentation in various modes of ministry has been a hallmark of those movements that have grown out of the Reformation period. The three standard versions of church governance within the Protestant movement, congregational, presbyterian, and episcopal, is strong evidence of this point.

Despite this clear philosophical and theological thrust and despite Protestantism's longstanding fidelity to the notion of the priesthood of all believers, local Protestant congregations are nonetheless susceptible to investing too much leadership responsibility in the person and the office of the pastor. This is not a mere rationalization for a pastor desiring fewer job responsibilities! Instead, it forms the theological foundation for a revisioning and consequent restructuring of ordained ministerial responsibilities within a local parish.

While I will spell this out in more detail later, suffice it to say for now that each congregation must ask the big questions that point to the congregation's work as ministers of the gospel. As example, we should ask not "How many homebound congregants can the pastor visit in a seven-day period?" but "What is our ministry as a church to the homebound in our congregation?" or "What can we as a community of faith do to reach out to those who need a visit?" This represents a shift in thinking, but unless a congregation is willing to confront that shift and explore it theologically, it will never restructure well. Without the necessary work of theological and ecclesiological reflection concerning the work of the local church, a congregation might just find itself cranky and frustrated that "our finances are bad and we can't afford a full-time minister."

More details coming as we move on . . .

Discussion Questions:

1. What is your assessment of the author's views on the changing role of the pastor?

2. What do you see as the downside of a part-time pastoral arrangement? Be specific.

2

A C H U R C H G O E S P A R T - T I M E

It is important to reiterate that in the ideal ecclesiastical world, under optimum circumstances, it is preferable that a church have a well-trained, full-time pastor on staff. As noted in the previous chapter, there is legitimate resistance to the notion of part-time ministry, and the reasons why will be addressed in this chapter and throughout this book. In fact, to frame the notion of effective part-time ministry within its proper overall context, it is important to detail why full-time ministry is indeed preferable wherever possible. My contention is that, in spite of the reality of the need for part-time ministry and the gifts available to the church through bivocational ministry, full-time pastoral service in a congregation remains the ideal if appropriate to a congregation's needs and resources.

In the best of worlds, a full-time pastor, an individual for whom the "job" of pastor is his or her primary source of income, provides the local church some kind of consistent safety net, presuming, of course, that she or he is doing the job well. The model of full-time ministry in the local parish assures that the congregation will receive what I will dub "standard pastoral services." Specifically, a parishioner can expect that his or her full-time minister will:

- Have set office hours; people in the congregation will know he or she is around the church a lot.

- Be easily accessible during "normal" working hours.

- Be available for pastoral emergencies as they arise.

- Be able to conduct funerals or attend to the dying during daytime working hours as necessary and usually be able to respond to any crisis within a very brief period of time.

- Stay "ahead of the curve" in terms of sermon preparation, denominational activities, and educational opportunities. It is common practice in many places that clergy luncheons, continuing education programs, and important denominational meetings meet during daytime working hours. On several occasions, as noted earlier, I have regretted being unable to attend a particular program that might be helpful to my own growth as a pastor because the ministry is not my full-time job. One can state quite accurately that the congregation will benefit from the pastor's access to educational and collegial growth opportunities. We will explore some reasons for that later on.

- Be available to interact with other members of the local neighborhood or the town and represent the church and its values in a social context beyond the boundaries of the local church.

- Be able to operate more proactively than reactively. A pastor's availability during the day provides the advantage of more time for planning, reflection, and collaboration with others with whom he or she ministers. While all of us in any job must be constantly prioritizing and reprioritizing, the bivocational pastor is more susceptible to being caught "putting out the heaviest fire" that is flaring within the congregation at any particular point. Generally speaking, the bivocational pastor does not have the time to do some of the legwork necessary for effective advanced planning to take place. The full-time pastor has more time for the kind of consultations that may lead to more productive formal meetings of boards and committees. This is especially true in those times when tensions arise and conflicts develop within members of the congregation.

- ⚬ Be more readily available for more meetings and for contact with different groups within the congregation.

- ⚬ In relatively small churches staffed by a solo pastor, the full-time clergyperson will have more flexibility to step in and provide programs as needs emerge or are identified within the community of faith. As a bivocational pastor, I have sensed the need to be engaged in the development and formation of youth ministry in my local church even to the point where I have led overnight retreats for our young people. While this experience has been among the most satisfying in my ministerial career and while much of my life experience is in youth ministry, the reality is that I have sometimes immediately followed a forty- to forty-five-hour week counseling in a public school with a Friday night engaged full tilt in the high-energy work of retreat leadership. All of this, of course, would occur as I also had to insure that I was doing justice to both my sermon and worship preparation and was available for pastoral calls as necessary. Every once in a while, all of these demands converge upon a bivocational minister in one concentrated period of time, as it has for me on many occasions over the years. Take away the forty- to forty-five hours in another job and I think you will see the difference, and the pastor will also experience a difference in the level of his or her personal fatigue!

- Provide educational programs at different hours. Personally, I think adult Christian education is among one of the most important facets of church life, and in our small church I place a high priority on incorporating it into our overall program. Yet I am only able to offer it on already packed Sunday mornings or during weeknights, while some other churches are able to offer breakfast or luncheon programs, often including book discussions. Make no mistake, the changing demographics of this nation mean that far fewer people are available at, say, noontime than in 1960! Nonetheless, there are still those who would prefer not to go out at night or who are at home during the day and could use a viable alternative to either the mall or *Days of Our Lives,* and a full-time pastorate is able to meet the needs of more people in a more flexible and multifaceted way.

- Be present to those members of the community who use the church building during the day. There really is something to be said for the witness value of this. When my youngest son was three and four, he attended a preschool program that rented space in our local Episcopal Church. Father Tom would often drop by and just say hi to the children on a fairly regular basis. The parents got to know and appreciate Father Tom and his kind, caring presence. Even though the preschool program had nothing to do with the church per se, it's clear that this particular priest was exercising a vital ministry on behalf of his congregation by simply being there. When I began considering a move from Roman Catholicism to a Protestant expression of Christianity, I turned to Father Tom for advice and counsel, all because I knew him through this program that happened to be housed in his church, during his work day.

Now, quite honestly, for a writer who is laying out a vision of a part-time, often bivocational pastorate, I think I have just made a pretty convincing case on behalf of full-time ministry. Nonetheless, a good (and growing!) number of churches, both traditionally small churches and those that have historically been larger but have found themselves in a downward attendance spiral, usually precipitating a financial spiral as well, have found themselves in positions in which they feel trapped:

- ⟿ They are experiencing financial difficulties clearly exacerbated by what has happened in the world around them.

- ⟿ When they examine their budget, they cannot avoid the conclusion that a huge percentage of their expenditures comes from paying their pastor.

This is often the great unspoken reality for many churches. Under the microscope of honest examination, they might realize that, regarding what they pay their minister, they have been operating in terms of what the church used to be rather than what it currently is. Some of my fellow clergy reading this book might quarrel with some of my implications. Some might argue, quite rightly, that even if this church that averaged one hundred people in worship ten years ago is now down to thirty-five, it still needs a full-time minister in order to be both proactive and continue to retain the best possible pastoral services. They might contend, rightly, that a pastor in this situation might need to spend more time on outreach and evangelism (the "e word"!![1]) in the community, perhaps seeking new, creative ways to reach out to the unchurched. They might argue that downsizing the minister's time would be highly counterproductive in terms of the church's mission and that the minister in this context might need to take more time doing those pastoral things less necessary in the church of the past. They might also say that even if people are not in church, there are numbers of congregants who are homebound or in nursing homes, unable to attend worship, yet who truly need the pastoral services their clergyperson could provide. In short, they might make a very convincing case that these declining numbers are a bit deceptive and that there is still full-time work to be done.

Now here is where the "rubber meets the road," because it is absolutely true that there is full-time work to be done! The community of the church is a full-time reality. When people assume membership in a church, they have freely bonded themselves to each other. This is the heritage we have received as evidenced in the writings of Paul, the message found in Acts of the Apostles, and the community of disciples Jesus gathered around himself! Here is where the larger question comes to the forefront: *What is the relationship between the full-time work of the local church and the actual job description of its pastor?* This is the point where questions build upon questions:

- If the church sees certain needs in the community as essential, does it necessarily follow that the pastor is the only one who can provide for those needs?

- In raising expectations for the pastor's ministerial obligations, have we unwittingly abdicated our theological heritage and actually downplayed or perhaps even buried our commitment to the priesthood of all believers?

What we are talking about is a church's openness to the process of reinterpretation. Is the church willing to honestly examine the assumptions under which it has been operating, perhaps for centuries? Is the local body of believers willing to think theologically and to engage in detailed, data-driven analysis of pastoral need, even to the point of seriously projecting into the future, as best as they are able? There is considerable information regarding church demographics all readily available to members of congregations.[2] The attendant question sits there as well: Is the pastor poised to help the church in this process of discernment, even as that process could lead to a reconfiguration of his or her role and compensation package? This, then, leads to the next question: Is the pastor willing to work side by side with her or his congregation even if doing so may cause the pastor to realize that he or she might have to seek church employment elsewhere? These are tough questions, and later on in this book I offer commentary regarding some of the ethical issues involved on the part of congregations in this situation. It seems obvious, though, that the work of interim pastors in many situations may very well include helping those local churches engage fully in this process of reinterpretation.

Here I offer a side note to pastors and seminarians: Each of us in the field of professional ministry must make some determinations of our own strengths and skills, the emerging needs of the church, and our own economic needs. Over the course of our professional lifetimes, we may find ourselves in situations in which serving our people may lead to decisions that are not in our economic best interest. This, however, is the heart of ministry, for we do follow the One who came not to be served, but to serve (see Matt. 20:28). In shaping our professional options in consultation with advisors, we all need to engage in honest exploration regarding the settings of ministry to which we are open. Some, out of skill and necessity, will always seek full-time positions. Others among us might be willing to explore a variety of configurations described in some detail in the next chapter.

In my view, the foundational question in the local church's reinterpretive process is how to distinguish between that which an entire church must do and that which is required of its pastor. Thus a starting point for reinterpretation would seem to be that a local church must identify the absolute essentials of its overall ministry, that is, those things that would need to get done even if its pastor were to walk off into the sunset a few minutes after concluding the Sunday service, with no plan whatsoever to return. In that intentionally absurd scenario, the church would be forced to come together and answer the questions: What needs to get done? What are our priorities?

My sense is that most churches would list the following, and probably more, necessities:

- Provide for good worship, education, and preaching, offering services that would inspire people to want to come to worship on Sundays and on other important occasions.

- Provide programming for youth and children, including an active youth ministry and Christian education program for children (church school or Sunday school).

- Make provisions for visiting those homebound, in nursing homes, and in hospitals on a consistent, ongoing basis.

- Ensure that pastoral care is provided to those seeking the assistance of the church.

- Be ready to respond to emergencies quickly, thoroughly, and well.

- Have an ongoing process of providing information to inquirers, newcomers and those seeking or considering baptism, confirmation, communion, or marriage within the Christian community.

- Make its presence known in its community; reach out to newcomers.

- Take care of the business expenses of the church and provide well for the physical plant (including ensuring that the plant will last well into the future).

- Think realistically about the church's future.

- Maintain connection and communication with its denomination and with other local churches of different faith traditions.

- Provide adequate "mission money" for those in need both locally and in other places where needs are glaring and timely.

Again, this is not an all-inclusive list. It is a solid educated guess about universal church priorities across cultures and denominations. It is here where this process of interpretation turns to the specific question: What does a church need from its pastor? In other words, where does the ministry of the pastor fit in to the overall ministry of the church? I would be really off base in trying to provide a "one size fits all" answer. Instead I pose the following questions:

- The great overriding question is: What on the previous list falls within the specific expertise of the pastor? Usual responses include preaching, planning for and presiding at worship, and providing pastoral care. Individual circumstances may vary; some pastors may have specific professional training and experience in Christian education, youth ministry, pastoral counseling, or church administration.

- What might be the unique skills of our current pastor or the skills we are seeking in a new pastor that would best meet our overall needs at this time?

- What tasks traditionally yielded to the pastor can we identify as more in keeping with the common goal of the overall church community? Usual answers include visiting the sick, staying in touch with the homebound, following up on the bereaved, and the like.

- In what ways can we be creative about how we go about doing ministry? At the risk of sounding trite, how willing are we to think "outside the box" of years of accrued traditions?

A church must then also ask some hard questions, questions alluded to in chapter 1, developed a bit further:

- What does the church expect of its pastor while he or she is in the office physically?

- Is the current church office hours configuration in the best interest of those who seek the services of the church?

- In a technological age, does the pastor need to communicate information to a church secretary, a webmaster, or people in key roles on boards and committees in person?

- Must the pastor be conversant in and comfortable with new technological modalities such as text messaging, e-mailing, the use of networking sites, and the like?

- Are we clinging to an old model of structuring in an age that offers and might even require new possibilities and approaches?

In raising these questions, a church must also be attentive to the potential downside in what appears to be "progress." There is a potential for depersonalization in following the technological path to its logical end, and I would never advocate for "cyber pastoring." While my own congregation and I like to kid each other about my propensity for technology, be it voice mail or text messaging, but especially e-mailing and blogging, please note that I said, "we kid each other," which implies real live relationships. It would be wrong to substitute an impersonal technological model for the "real time" human exchanges and interactions that are a part of pastoral life. Many of us, in our nonchurch professions, myself included, have experienced technological communication run amok, to the point that people in offices right next to each other send loaded e-mails rather than communicating face to face. In spite of increased technological communication in schools, I have noticed a slight increase in parental requests for meetings. One colleague pointed out to me that it's possible that the increase in technological communication has actually produced a hunger for real live human contact. Interesting point! I have also seen this technological explosion spill over to the local parish scene as e-mail correspondence substitutes for interaction at established church meetings. This can become counterproductive to doing the church's work and, most especially, to strengthening the relational foundations of a religious community —those ties that bind us each to the other!

While that old song from *Casablanca* most certainly holds true and "the fundamental things apply, as time goes by,"[3] it nevertheless makes complete sense for the church to ask the hard questions that will lead to both varied answers and different ministerial configurations based on the unique needs of each local congregation.

The question of how to structure the pastor's role in the local congregation always flows from deeper questions that each congregation must answer. Current church reality has most certainly put many local churches in the position in which raising these questions is both necessary and ultimately inevitable. If a local church happens to conclude that it is time to move away from a full-time pastor model and to consider calling a bivocational minister, it must proceed to face what that really means, for there is more than one way to be part-time or bivocational. The next chapter attempts to explain this in more detail.

Discussion Questions

1. Some would argue that a church that employs a part-time pastor will inevitably sacrifice the quality of pastoral care, preaching, amd overall ministry. What are your thoughts?

2. Please comment on the author's views regarding the reinterpretation he describes.

3

PART-TIME AND BIVOCATIONAL
What Are We Talking About?

The United Church of Christ ministerial profile asks the question of the local church regarding whether the church is willing to allow its pastor to seek part-time employment so as to supplement his or her income. A review of published employment opportunities in this and other denominations indicates that many churches are willing to consider part-time pastors or those who might be bivocational. A glimpse at the November 2009 "United Church Employment Opportunities"[1] indicates that in some states the majority of current openings for pastors fall under the aegis of part-time. Some individuals and denominations, such as the Presbyterian Church, USA, have appropriated the language of the "tent-making pastor," a reference to the ministry of Paul as described in scripture.[2] Dennis Bickers has written a significant work on this subject that goes by that specific title.[3] Some denominations have had a considerable history of bivocational ministry, including Southern Baptists. In the late 1980s Luther Dorr published an important work on the topic that referred extensively, though not exclusively, to the experience of that denomination with respect to this approach to local church leadership.[4]

It is important to understand that a pastor who is something other than full-time is not in a "one size fits all" role. In fact, one of the first decisions a church has to make should it be open to the possibility of part-time ministry has to do with the particular configuration of that leadership model. Likewise, prospective pastors, including seminarians who might consider part-time, bivocational ministry as part of their future, must understand that the term does not mean the same thing in all circumstances. In this chapter I list and explore several different operative configurations. I attempt in the process to spell out specific expectations inherent in each. My suggestion is that a church and its search committees, diocesan and synodal officials, placement officers, and prospective part-time ministers use these descriptors as a starting point for further questioning and dialogue:

MODEL #1: *Pastor employed full-time elsewhere, part-time in the church.*

Quite frankly, this is the model I know best. This has been my life in the almost nine years I have served as an ordained clergyperson in the United Church of Christ. Though I was not a pastor in the Roman Catholic Church, it was likewise my experience as a highly involved Roman Catholic clergyperson for the nine years I served as an ordained deacon. In chapter 4, I will discuss the Catholic concept of diaconate in relationship to bivocational issues and questions within Protestant denominations.

The church willing to employ its pastor under this model has to come to terms with the fact that, generally speaking, full-time work is both time and energy consuming. Unless the church is calling someone who works late shifts in his or her primary profession, the usual configuration renders a pastor as not "on site" during the workday. While the specifics of this depend on the particular full-time job the clergyperson holds, the reality is that the other job will more than likely both take up more time and pay the minister more money. Likewise, the minister's full-time employer has legitimate expectations that the pastor is going to provide his or her primary supervisor with a full-time commitment and that ministerial obligations will not get in the way of his or her job performance.

In employing a pastor otherwise employed, a church also has to explore the attitude of the primary employer to the needs that may arise in parish ministry. In some jobs it would be virtually impossible for one to leave during the day to get to a hospital, arrive at the scene of some other kind of crisis, or conduct a funeral. Later in this book, we get into more detail concerning the really hard questions surrounding these issues. In addition, the pastor in this situation has to reach an honest assessment based on his or her understanding of work conditions, relationship with one's primary employer, and ability to manage both time and fatigue.

I will cite my situation as a living example of this approach to bivocationality while fully understanding that it is not all encompassing, that is, it is specific to my concrete life experience. Nonetheless, I hope and I trust that it might provide a lens through which the reader might be able to look at the unique situation regarding the potential for bivocational work within the context of a particular congregation. I am hopeful also that this anecdotal disclosure might prompt worthwhile questioning on the part of prospective bivocational pastors and those who might seek to call them.

As I have mentioned, I work as a full-time school counselor (popularly and traditionally known as guidance counselor) in a public school system. Throughout the more than nine years I have served as pastor of a small church, I have also held this full-time position. My work in public schools is my primary source of income. It is also the job through which I receive my health and dental insurance, and it is the position that will eventually provide me the bulk of my retirement income. The fact of these benefits is no minor one as we shall see in considering the financial implications of calling and hiring a part-time pastor.

A school counselor leads a busy life. Some school days can be what I'd call energy intensive. Simple translation: you get home exhausted! Depending on the given day, one might be swimming in reams of college recommendations, dealing with angry parents, spending hours in meetings, playing middle person between teachers and parents, administrators and students, and other individuals or groups who might be in conflict with one another. Putting it as succinctly and clearly as I can: It is a full-time job, no ifs, ands, or buts!

The church in which I have been serving is the one and only church in Connecticut's smallest town. While the town is composed of about 750 people and the church membership stands at a relatively small 107, it is a busy and active community. Serving as pastor of this church has required a great deal of energy as well. One of the first issues a part-time pastor needs to confront is found in the title he or she holds. The individual called to serve a church is expected to serve as the church's pastor. It would be easy for people in my situation to see his or her role primarily as providing worship and preaching on Sundays and emergency pastoral services as needed, with the occasional celebration of a baptism or a wedding mixed in—more of a chaplaincy role than that of the more encompassing role covered in the designation of "pastor."

The danger in this minimalist approach is that the individual and the church that would be comfortable with the person functioning in this manner would fail to understand that the church needs an involved and active pastor, someone who is fully engaged in the total life of the church. In other words, part-time pastoring has to take into account that once you accept the responsibilities of the pastoral position, though your hours may indeed be part-time, though you may devote the majority of your time to your full-time position, you are always the pastor of that church so long as you and the church are in relationship with each other. "Part-time" may refer to the hours spent. It does not refer to one's pastoral focus. If one chooses this position, one chooses to be the church's pastor, twenty-four hours a day, seven days a week. Period!

In later chapters, we will get very specific in terms of possible ways to structure bivocational, part-time ministry. At this point, however, it is worth pointing out some of the specific ways in which the congregation in Union and I have worked out this arrangement. Thus I will provide a listing of some of the key elements of our approach.

We make maximum use of my available time on site Sunday mornings. Interestingly, the day on which I am writing these words is a Sunday. When I get to church today, the day I am writing this material, I will meet with a group of Sunday schoolers to plan something at worship and will also have a session with our Confirmation students. This is a rather light Sunday. In other weeks, I might be part of our monthly deacons' meeting, lead an adult education session either before or after worship, attend a congregational meeting or potluck luncheon, or hold a counseling session or meeting with parents of children to be baptized or with an engaged couple. In other words, every Sunday is a busy Sunday.

My congregation and I communicate a lot through technological means. I make extensive use of e-mail to check in on parishioners and to do a plethora of information sharing and organizational tasks. Our church does not have a secretary so a lot of worship planning, consultation with musicians, and arrangements for meetings comes via cyberspace. In addition, I have an extensive e-mail list of parishioners and those who have come into contact with our church, and I send out e-mails at least once a week regarding upcoming church activities. In recent years, I have instituted, in addition to our website (which is rather good, and now really evolving in different directions), an interactive blog that provides an opportunity for me to introduce and follow up on topics we have talked about or will talk about at worship. Parenthetically, it has also become a great source of outreach to those who are not directly connected to our congregation.

From the beginning of my work in this church, this congregation has not required either that I conduct set office hours or that I give any quantitative accounting of exactly how many hours I work each week. This topic is a rather controversial one, I have discovered, that needs to be address by local congregations and their search committees. As we will see, there are congregations that insist on some combination of both in terms of maintaining clear access and accountability. In speaking from my experience in Union, I will say that in order for the model in which I have operated to work well, the foundational element needed is trust. I am talking about the congregation's trust in both the pastor's competence and the fact that he or she will schedule time well so as to meet the needs of the congregation. In speaking about and analyzing myself, I think it is a fair to say that my congregation knows, via my e-mails and the energy I bring when present among them, that, day in and day out, whether I am on site in Union or in front of my computer, I am always working as their pastor. I fully understand how some churches would worry that the model under which I have been operating can lead to what amounts to an absentee pastor. What I am saying is that, handled properly with high levels of communication all around, it might even free the pastor to get more work done than in a traditional "count the hours" system. The key to success in this approach is that the pastor has to identify what needs to be done in the church at this time given his or her pastoral skills and then proceed to plan time accordingly. Note that the emphasis, then, is less on time spent and more on the tasks that need to be done. This shift in emphasis requires considerable time management skills and the pastor's capability to establish priorities.

I emphasize both to our deacons and to others active in the congregation that I need to be kept abreast of pastoral needs regarding those who would benefit from a home visit or some other pastoral call. It is important that I am informed concerning who is in the hospital, who is going through difficulty, and so on. The fact that I live thirty minutes away from the town whose church I serve compounds matters, but with the emphasis on communication permeating the pastoral relationship, this distance need not be an impediment to good pastoral ministry.

I have a good working relationship with the local funeral home, and in working with families to set arrangements they are well aware of my time constraints and limitations. Quite honestly, this, along with urgent pastoral emergencies, is an area that can be highly problematic for any bivocational pastor. In this case, to put it directly, what happens if, because of family needs, the service absolutely has to be at 11 in the morning, which runs smack into the heart of one's full-time workday? This direct conflict has not been something with which I have had to deal. The very nature of the small church makes it unlikely that one encounters this kind of conflict very often at all.

Generally speaking, the number of funerals that occur in small churches do not really rival the number that occur in larger congregations. I have also found that most families try to accommodate schedules, including that of the clergyperson. In addition, with our increasingly mobile society, it is hard for some families to gather relatives from afar for a mid-week, midday service as well. This is one of those societal shifts that has had impact upon the practices of the local church. Yet this is not to say that a real conflict could never happen! While my experience has been less than problematic, the potential for disaster does exist, and this is a topic about which search committees, churches, and ministers need to be clear as they consider the models we are describing and their applicability to their own local churches. It is a topic that must be addressed satisfactorily before a bivocational pastor and a church agree to enter a pastoral relationship with each other.

I have made clear to members of my congregation that I want to be called if they need me right away. Here I am talking about hospital or home visits with those who are dying or with the recently bereaved. My cell phone number is widely published in the congregation and I pride myself in accessibility. My part-time status is respected by parishioners, and my experience has been that I am not called upon arbitrarily or capriciously, only in times of real need. As with the funeral issue, this is most certainly an area that could cause conflict. In the worst-case scenario, one that has not yet occurred, a minister would have to have open, honest communication with his or her primary employer. The reality is that anyone who holds a job might find himself or herself in the unique situation of having to go to an employer to explain the need to take a little time off. Many employers grant their employees personal leave and employers with good will traditionally make exception for individual circumstances. Having said all of this is no assurance that there will never be any conflict. It is more an assertion that the very worst-case scenario is more rare exception than norm.

I try to make clear, and attempted to do so from the beginning of my call, that this church is a priority in my life and that I will devote heart and soul to it, its issues, and its future. I like to think that while my parishioners realize that I have another job, they also see me as fully engaged in ministry with them and that there may even be times when they might forget that I am employed elsewhere. This "forgetfulness" is good in that it indicates that the pastor is approaching the congregation as a full-time church. On the other hand, the congregation, for a lot of reasons, also has to be cognizant of the limitations of part-time work as well.

The pastor and church willing to engage in the relationship encompassed by this model also need to be willing to subject themselves to ongoing reflection and communication. For personal reasons, at the time I entered the ordained ministry of the United Church of Christ, I had to choose this model were I to have the opportunity to serve as a local church pastor. It was not time for me to retire from public education and enter full-time ministry. My past experience as a highly involved Roman Catholic permanent deacon (see chapter 4) helped me on a lot of levels in preparing for and implementing this ministerial approach. My experience has taught me that it is doable and exciting and, most importantly, can be an approach that serves the local church well, under the proper conditions.

MODEL #2: *Pastor employed primarily as a pastor with less than full-time salary and holding a part-time job as well.*

Some congregations that have traditionally employed full-time ministers might consider making a decision that would downsize the position to one defined as a three-quarter or two-thirds position. For the individual who needs full-time employment, this arrangement puts one in the situation whereby he or she must seek part-time work that does not conflict with church obligations. I am aware of some congregations that have scaled back to this part-time arrangement with the promise that their intent is to return eventually to the full-time model, usually attached to the caveat of the church finances getting better, and with that expectation even built into the terms of the agreement between the church and its pastor.

This model poses unique challenges for the pastor. First of all, many of the same conflicts described in the first model with respect to potential time conflict are present in this situation. Granting that the key distinction between the two is the full-time nature of the other job in Model # 1, there may still be times when the job conflict comes into play. After all, even in this model, the part-time employer expects the employee to be present and to fulfill responsibilities related to that particular job.

Likewise, the pastor faces the dilemma of finding adequate part-time employment. He or she will have to determine potential work venues and deal with the adequacy of wages and time conflicts within those possible positions. The pastor will also have to determine the importance of the interrelatedness of his or her two jobs. One might, for example, seek part-time employment in a related field—for example, teaching some courses, doing part-time chaplaincy or counseling, or taking on some kind of consulting work. On the other hand, the minister may opt for a job that provides steady, predictable hours in an area completely unrelated to his or her professional training as a clergyperson—perhaps retail, sales, or the like. Depending on the individual, he or she might find the position outside the church either rewarding because of its difference from the demands of pastoral work or a frustrating use of one's time, albeit necessary to supplement one's income.

In this arrangement, the inevitable issue of health-care benefits arises as well. Part-time employers are less likely to offer adequate health care packages. I would strongly suggest that the candidate faced with this situation negotiate with a potential church employer to find the best possible benefits package, including provisions for future retirement. It strikes me that this is a significant issue of justice for congregations who also happen to be employers. Many church people are inclined to run away from that designation as it smacks of worldliness and may not seem churchy enough. They may even find themselves enthusiastic about what they see as a reduced responsibility to provide a comprehensive benefits package to their part-time employee. The reality is that the living out of social justice ideals espoused from the pulpit applies directly to the fairness with which a church treats its employees, in this case, its pastor!

Ongoing communication between the pastor and a designated pastoral relations committee or other appropriate representative group in the church is extremely important should a church choose to call a pastor under this arrangement. Especially in the case of the church that has downsized, the designation of time as, for example, three-quarters, carries with it an expectation that the pastor will be present in the congregation quite often. There would tend as well to be less flexibility about the matter of office hours. It would be very easy for something that is technically a scaled-down arrangement to remain in practice a full-time job. It is also quite possible that the congregation might be frustrated when the pastor refers to the specific part-time nature of the position especially if that reflects either a change in job description or a pre-ferred temporary solution. My sense, in reviewing employment data in various denominations at the time of this writing and in anecdotal conversations with fellow pastors, church officials, and search committee members whom I have known, is that there is and will be an increase in churches moving toward this arrange-ment. This most certainly will continue to lead to some complex and challenging situations that prospective churches and candi-dates must face openly and head on.

MODEL # 3: *Pastor serving half time as a pastor and working in another job half time as well.*

Many of the circumstances described in analyzing the second model operate here also. Concern about the benefits package is even more acute in this particular model. The clear-cut part-time nature of the pastoral position outlined here would seem to di-minish some of the concerns regarding hours at the church and the like that are confronted in the case of the pastor who is defined as having this ministerial position as a primary job. There are practical questions regarding what possible jobs could comple-ment the lifestyle required of a pastor and all of the attendant job pressures that would be operative in both positions. If anything, the problems described in the first two models are really compounded!

MODEL # 4: *Pastor serves as a part-time pastor at two or more different churches.*

This approach, which is not uncommon and has been operative in many congregations for a good while, carries with it the drawbacks found in other approaches as well as its own unique one. The pastor who opts for this arrangement runs the risk that he or she will be perceived as spending more time at one church than the other(s). This perception that the pastor has a primary and a secondary church in this arrangement can be quite crippling. In addition to all of the time management and communication skills required to navigate the other part-time models, the pastor in this situation may need to find ways to bring the congregations together from time to time and to help establish a good relationship between or among them.

These four models do not exhaust all of the possibilities for part-time ministry. Another option would be the stand-alone, part-time position in which the pastor either does not work a second job or might be spending time as a student. It is here where the role of the student pastor comes into play. It's possible that I may also have left some other possibilities out, though I think these examples are rather all encompassing. What is crucially important to realize is that in any part-time arrangement, the needs of the church continue to exist as full-time needs. While it is important for reasons of fairness and often for good emotional health that the minister stay within the boundaries of the contract, it is also necessary to understand that the congregation is responsible for insuring that ministry is done well within the congregation. Thus none of these models can work if they are accompanied by the theological perspective that ministry belongs solely or primarily in the territory of the ordained. I emphasize once again that a full appreciation for the ministerial responsibilities of the congregation is not only a pragmatic consideration in a changing religious landscape, but it is also good theology!

It is my expectation that many reading this book are considering or studying for careers as ordained clergy in their denominations. I am hopeful also that this work is being examined by those who teach these prospective pastors and by denominational officials and placement officers. It is important that the seminarian/candidate for ministry understand the multiplicity of options for structuring a leadership role that is both operative and emerging in the contemporary and future church. Whereas there once was a time when a seminarian would expect to come out of seminary and receive a call as a full-time pastor, the expectations these days are quite different for many. With the increase in ordained ministry as a second career, a good number of individuals are now coming out of seminaries in the middle ages of their lives and may be open to work arrangements that do not require full-time commitment. It is important, then, that students and their leaders understand the unique set of circumstances attached to the various models of part-time or bivocational ministry.

In a similar vein, serious attention has to be paid to the matter of adequate educational preparation. This would be operative on two levels. Quite obvious is what we have just discussed—the uniqueness of the varied options must be explored thoroughly. Even more crucial, however, is that denominations and local congregations need to insure that part-time ministers will receive an outstanding theological education and that those congregations who call them will not be shortchanged and destined to have pastoral leaders with inferior theological and pastoral skills training.

This gets quite complex for several reasons. It is quite possible that people interested in ministry who are considering changing careers may still be working and may find it difficult to enroll in a full-time three-year Master of Divinity program in order to fulfill the professional degree requirements. Given the stressors and time constraints in their lives and their recognition that the salary they will receive will be considerably less than that of a full-time clergyperson, individuals may question whether they need this particular degree in order to be a pastoral leader, especially in a small church. Congregations may find themselves questioning this as well and acknowledging that if they are going to just be paying part-time wages, it's perfectly acceptable to lower educational expectations.

I wish to approach this subject from a different angle. Here I will freely state what some might derisively call a bias. I prefer instead to acknowledge it as a conviction, a strong belief that at this point in American religious history, we need to strengthen what we might describe as the mainstream, mainline church and the local congregations of that church. I am talking about churches within those denominations that have been identified as the ones suffering from declining enrollment over the past two decades. These denominations and the local churches within them, oftentimes the churches on the green and the old neighborhood churches in many American towns, have fallen behind the evangelical, fundamentalist, and nondenominational and interdenominational churches that dot the landscape of our nation, trailing them in attendance indicators, financial stability, and variety of program offerings.

I write from a perspective of a United Church of Christ pastor convinced that American Christianity needs churches that are small, progressive, and alive. While I would expect that many conservative, evangelical, and fundamentalist Christians may glean good information and suggestions from this work, I want to make clear that I am convinced that American Christianity will benefit from the bolstering and renewal of such denominations as the United Church of Christ; Disciples of Christ; the Episcopal Church; the United Methodists; the Evangelical Lutheran Church in America; the Presbyterian Church, USA; the Reformed Church in America; American Baptist Churches USA; the Moravian Church; and those several others that meet the definition of mainline American churches.

The overwhelming preponderance of those considering bivocational and/or part-time parish work will serve small churches. It is because of the size of these churches and the financial limitations due to size that they are unable to pay full-time salaries. In my view, maintaining strong and active small churches ought to be a priority of denominational leadership. In order for larger churches to be successful, they have to establish smaller communities within them. Small churches have the built-in advantage that comes from congregations for whom there is much familiarity among the members. Close-knit congregations have their drawbacks too, among which include a tendency toward exclusivity and a natural inclination to be somewhat suspicious of outsiders. It is in this regard that the larger church needs the small church, especially the well-established church of considerable heritage in its neighborhood or town, to be welcoming and hospitable to those outside its ranks.

Many of the conservative churches have been in the forefront of opposition to marriage equality and/or civil rights protection for homosexuals. They have forged reputations among marginalized members of their communities as being less than inviting. It is my strong belief that the mainline church has the potential to be a voice for an inclusive, welcoming Christian vision in neighborhoods and towns. This is important both in terms of proclaiming the gospel to those who may benefit from hearing it and because all members of congregations benefit when this all-embracing understanding of Christianity is highlighted as part of the mission of the church. I think that people of all ages, but quite notably the young, need to know that Christianity need not be associated as the property of those opposed to social progress or to science and reason. Therefore small churches need pastors who have been the beneficiaries of strong theological education and have been trained in programs in which they have been exposed to strong, accurate biblical research and the complexities and nuances of theological thinking, all in proper historical perspective.

Conservative churches of all sizes, pointedly exemplified by megachurches, have been highly successful in providing for the needs of their people on many levels. Progressive small churches face the challenge of attempting to do so as well. A recent visit and conversation with a search committee chairperson in a small Connecticut town with which I was familiar from my childhood highlights this point. In this particular church, the congregation maintains a beautiful sanctuary, which in the post–World War II heyday of mainline American religion would have been filled on a regular basis, at least according to what I've been told about the "good old days" in that place! In 2009, this church, which could comfortably house over two hundred people at worship, averaged about thirty-five at every service. This shift in attendance, coupled with increased heating costs, led to a reduction of services held in the now cavernous sanctuary during the cold weather months which, in turn, led to peoples' sense of loss that they weren't able to experience worship in their quite beautiful and historic sanctuary.

Meantime, down the road sits a fairly newly established evangelical interdenominational church that packs its several services each weekend, has a separate building to provide for the recreational needs of its young people, and conducts a variety of programs reaching out to all demographic groups within its geographical range—programs for parents, school children, senior citizens, families, the divorced, the addicted, and so on. People in the established church on the town green readily bemoan the fact that things are not the way they used to be and that they just can't do things the way "these newfangled churches can." They often express great concern that the congregation is aging and that other churches have exhibited more success than theirs in reaching that "middle group" of potential congregants, people usually in their thirties and forties, oftentimes the parents of children.

Mainline Christianity needs to bolster these small mainline churches by shedding any remnant of a hopeless, can't-do attitude. It is anything but desirable to wallow in pity or to wring one's hands and take on a constantly complaining approach. Instead it is important to acknowledge what these evangelical churches do well and to understand that because their theological foundations are different from the mainline approach, they will emphasize certain aspects of ministry that would be less important or maybe not even important at all to, for example, a middle-of-the-road congregation of the United Church of Christ.

The contemporary evangelical church, large, small, and in between, has been very successful at building what I would call an "alternative universe" based on a worldview that conflicts with much of what mainstream America accepts. As a result of the theological mindset they embrace and espouse, they seek to provide alternatives within their congregations to the institutional realities of mainstream life. This is particularly true, though not limited to, what these churches offer children and youth. Since many conservative Christians are suspicious of public schools, the sex education received there, and the way these schools have embraced what conservatives would derisively call "moral relativism" and "secular humanism," the local evangelical church provides both alternative education and, through their highly developed youth ministry programs, a well-structured means for social interaction that will often outdo anything the public school can offer. Many of the high school students whom I counsel in the public school setting have told me about the well-organized programs for young people in their churches that they have attended, programs that often tackle issues they believe public education has either ignored or taught improperly. These churches often provide great social opportunities for both young people and their families and serve as support networks for the home schooling many of the children in their congregations receive in reaction to the perceived evils of public education. For adults as well, these churches offer a reliable refuge from what they see as the darkness and sinfulness of the world. Much to their credit, many of these churches have poured enormous money and provided staffing for a variety of programs that have been helpful to adults on their life journey, such as divorce recovery groups, single parent groups, men and women's Bible study, and the like. They have even become wonderful networking places for those seeking to reenter the dating scene and meet a potential partner of the opposite sex.

These congregations tend to take seriously the importance of being responsible in one's stewardship and in giving financially to the church. For many of them, the biblical notion of tithing 10 percent of one's income is a fact of congregational life. Of all the possible ways to spend one's money outside of one's self and family, there is no more important cause to these individuals than giving to the ministries of their church.

Mainline Christians, whether we dub them moderates or progressives, tend to look at these issues differently and in reality have a different theological mindset. Rather than seeing the "world" as intrinsically evil and public schools as valueless institutions, mainline Christians tend to acknowledge the necessary distinctions between church and state, see the limitations of what public schools can do, and often applaud their efforts in the areas of both diversity and health education. For a great number of mainstream Christians, it is important that their children be taught tolerance of the "alternate lifestyles" that evangelicals might lament as sinful and condemned by the Bible. Mainline Christians are less inclined to appropriate a literal interpretation of the biblical injunctions about tithing and tend to recognize that, in an individual or family's life, the church is not the only worthwhile cause to which one might give. The necessity of fulfilling a 10 percent requirement because it is "biblical law" tends not to be uppermost within this approach to Christianity.

These different understandings of theology thus lead to contrasting expectations of what the local church ought to do. Suffice it to say that a great number of conservative Christian churches have done an outstanding job providing good services inspired by the theological positions that are important in their collective lives. Even as mainline Christians quarrel, as I most certainly will, with some of those underpinnings, we must acknowledge that many of these churches provide top-of-the-line preaching in terms of communication skills and engagement and well-developed educational and musical material, all within the parameters of their theological leanings.

Prior to speaking with a search committee in a church that was in the process of beginning the interview process for a new pastor, I was interested in trying to figure out the causes for their decline in church attendance over the past decade. One night, I took a ride through their town and discovered a fairly new looking church just about a mile down the street from this established church in the town's center. When I got home, I scurried to my computer to this other church's website and there discovered a local congregation that offered "something for everybody" and that went out of their way to advertise the praise band that was a feature of their regular contemporary music services. In reading through this site, one could readily see that they placed great emphasis in presenting Christianity toward those who had little or no church background and that they engaged in a sustained, deliberate attempt to reach the young. Although they were a congregation of a long-established denomination, they completely downplayed their denominational ties and could have easily been mistaken for a nondenominational church. The established mainline church on the town green bemoaned the fact that their youth group, so active a generation ago, did not exist, and yet here was this other church offering youth retreats, camping opportunities, and a full plate of social and recreational gatherings that actually drew as participants members of the mainline church, who would attend the other church's events with their friends. My sense is that many of those young people would not have been terribly cognizant of the theological differences espoused by either of these two churches.

Sad as it is to say, many mainline churches have given up on youth ministry, yielding to a mindset that our youth are not really interested in being connected to a church and that the period of adolescence, with its developmental task of questioning authority and institutions, is a time in which young people are going to naturally stray away from anything that smacks of religion. It is my conviction, as someone who has been involved in youth ministry for most of my professional life, that if one is looking at the full range of needs in a full-time church, staffed by a part-time pastor or not, one must take youth ministry off the back burner and bring it up front, not by poorly imitating what conservative churches do well, but by instead providing programs built on the theological strengths of the mainline denominational traditions represented within those churches.

In the same way, the small church, strapped for funds or not, has an obligation to offer the very best worship opportunities available. This does not mean that to do so one must seek to imitate the new-fangled methodologies of the megachurches and those smaller conservative churches. Doing worship well in mainline churches does not mean finding a way to beat those praise bands at their own game. Instead it means to take seriously the importance of good, innovative, creative worship built on the theological and liturgical foundations of that church tradition and to see this prioritization as one of the full-time needs of the local church.

In summary then, it is vital that moderate and progressive mainline congregations work tirelessly to provide services that meet the full range of need, all the while maintaining theological integrity and a commitment to the ideals that mark their approach to the Christian gospel. In offering programs that incorporate the best in contemporary methodologies and that draw from a wide range of sources, including what the conservative churches do well, local congregations should not abandon their denominational identities. Instead they need to find new ways to communicate those identities to those whom they welcome into their midst, be they unchurched, young, those considering returning to church, or simply people who are new in town. The bottom line is that local towns and neighborhoods need these churches to provide:

- ❧ Sound theological education for adults and young people alike.
- ❧ Good worship with preaching that respects human reason and knowledge.
- ❧ Excellent church music.
- ❧ Programs that meet the physical and spiritual needs of the congregation and provide an outlet in which to engage in Christian action on behalf of justice.
- ❧ Social opportunities for people of all ages.
- ❧ Educational and social programming that reflects the inclusive, welcoming gospel vision these churches embrace.
- ❧ Valuable opportunities for intergenerational participation in the overall life of the church.

Good theological training for pastors has always been an antidote to a Christianity based on whim, prejudice, or a lack of historical perspective. This tension between "uneducated" preachers who "received the call of the Spirit" and those formally educated in theological schools has been part of our country's religious history, most evident through the period of the Second Great Awakening and beyond.[5] The emergence of a necessity for part-time or bivocational pastors in our current day has brought this tension back to light. Dennis Bickers, who has done much work on the topic of bivocational ministry, acknowledges the need for pastors to receive a theological education but is also quite comfortable with churches calling pastors who do not, especially in light of his concern for the "liberal" tendencies of some seminaries. Bickers actually pastored a church himself without benefit of a college degree.[6]

I have difficulty with that. I believe that for someone to be a pastor, he or she has to have a background grounded in serious study of philosophy, theology, liberal arts, counseling, church music, and biblical research, coupled with supervised practicum experiences so that one may grow in pastoral skill. During his or her time spent pastoring a church, the minister will be confronted with serious questions concerning the most complex issues known to humankind: Why does suffering happen? Why does a good God permit evil? What happens after death? Why do innocent people suffer? And many, many more. A solid academic grounding and relevant practical experiences provide the necessary knowledge for dealing with these matters, especially with respect to learning what one should not say in certain situations, especially around, though not limited to, death and dying.

Local congregations and denominational officials also need to realize that the local pastor is representative of the denomination and its theological heritage. While usually not ranked as important as good preaching, worship, pastoral care, the work of a pastor in explaining the church's denominational heritage, and helping people within the flock come to a deepened understanding of their tradition are important tasks for a pastor. That will only occur if pastoral leadership has a strong theological grounding. Welcoming new members, explaining denominational history, and having a well-grounded and working understanding of comparative Christianity and world religions are important components of qualitative pastoral skill. They are some of the essential full-time needs of the church that must not be compromised. An Episcopal congregation, for example, needs assurance that its rector knows well and can communicate the heart and the nuances of Episcopal faith and tradition to those who inquire and to those within the congregation who raise questions or who take stands on various issues that arise. Even if you are a part-time pastor, you serve a full-time church and one of its full-time needs will be good, well-grounded teaching from its pastor!

The flip side of this coin is that denominational leaders need to be creative in structuring opportunities for potential ministers to receive academic and pastoral training. Considering the emergence of second career ministry candidates and the growth in part-time opportunities, I have to wonder if the traditional track of three years at a seminary/theological school in order to earn the MDiv degree is the best way to provide the necessary education for pastoral ministry. The clear preference of denominational officials has been to have candidates train on that particular track. Over the last few years, there has been an increased willingness to look at alternate routes in order to achieve the same goal.

Let me share my experience with a denominational candidacy committee back in 1998 and 1999. I have great regard for the theological underpinning of that denomination and for the people with whom I came into contact as I considered pursuing ministry within that church tradition. To make a long story short, this particular committee was insistent that were I to qualify for ordination in this church, I would have to go off and spend a full year in residence at one of the denomination's seminaries, all of which were at a good distance from my home. I was troubled that one highly placed official within that denomination told me that the gospel often calls us to leave our families behind for "the sake of the Kingdom." I had to get my bearings and be sure I was speaking to a product of the Reformation, for I had long heard that argument as justification for mandatory clerical celibacy in the church in which I was raised!

As the father of three young children at the time and as someone with a full-time job, I found this to be impractical. I knew that even when I would eventually get ordained, I would be spending a good number of years in bivocational, part-time ministry. Yet that fact in itself should not have absolved me from academic responsibilities. I believed then, as I do now, that the church needs well-educated pastors. My concern was that I had a strong theological background and in addition to a graduate degree and years teaching theology, I also was an ordained clergyman in another Christian tradition. I articulated the position that an alternative approach would be to find the gaps in my educational and pastoral background and from that point establish a program of rigorous academic work, including challenging courses at top-notch institutions (I proposed coursework at Yale, Lutheran School of Theology, Chicago, Andover Newton Theological School, and Harvard). I also thought I would benefit from an in-depth field education experience as I recognized that I needed both immersion in and reflection upon the lived experience of functioning in a different Christian denomination. In honesty, I was extremely disappointed in what I thought was the narrow focus of this denomination's approach, one that contrasted with that taken by the association committee on ministry in the denomination in which I have been serving throughout this decade.

It is my understanding that denominations are exhibiting more flexibility now than some of them may have in 1999. It is also my belief that they must maintain stringent guidelines even as they consider alternate educational paths so they insure that the desirable goals they espouse are reached. As I see it, second career, bivocational and part-time ministers should be required to have an outstanding academic background, because the stakes out there are very high. The small church is uniquely positioned to provide a viable mainline approach to the proclamation of the Christian gospel, lending a voice that serves, in my observation, as a necessary alternative to a more conservative approach that often downplays the importance of human reason and conscience as gifts from God.[7] If our small churches are to be well equipped in the communities in which they are established, if they are to stand well in the long line of the Christian heritage they represent, if they are to serve the full needs of those in this world whose lives might intersect with the life of the church, they need pastors whose training will be inferior to none, pastors well equipped to meet the many needs of a demanding full-time church.

Discussion Questions:

1. What are the pros and cons involved in each of the models of part-time ministry the author describes?

2. Comment on the author's assertions regarding mainline churches in comparison with more "evangelical" churches. What has been your experience with mainline churches in relation to the issues he raises? What is the situation in your local community or neighborhood with respect to these issues?

3. Comment on the author's statements regarding the importance of quality theological education for part-time clergy.

4

T H E   B I V O C A T I O N A L   M I N I S T E R

While much of the discussion regarding bivocational ministry has centered on the part-time nature of the minister's job and how part-time ministry can serve the needs of a congregation, it is also important to look at this topic and explore it from an entirely different angle. It is worth examining the benefits and drawbacks of having a bivocational minister in the context of what it means to actually be a bivocational minister. Now, if you are inclined to say that we have already done so in the pages that proceeded this one, I wish to suggest that while we have looked at the stressors in the life of someone trying to do professional ministry and also another job, and while we have documented the concerns that a congregation might have with such a pastoral arrangement, we have not even begun to explore what it means to be a pastor in this situation and how one's bivocational status might affect the way one is able to function as a pastor.

In this chapter, I will attempt to address these issues and will draw on my prior experience as a Roman Catholic permanent deacon as a source for both background and comparison. First, I'd like to state the obvious. A pastor who is bivocational and whose other income is not church-related spends a considerable amount of time working in a position in which he or she is seen by others primarily for what he or she does on that job. Unless the minister reveals to someone that he or she also is an ordained clergyperson or unless, for some reason, that fact is public knowledge, the clergyperson functions on that job evaluated upon that job performance and in relationship with others through the professional and social networks that accompany that other occupation.

In these facts alone we find a significant and considerable difference in the lives of many bivocational ministers compared with those of full-time professional pastors. For the full-timer, ministry and job are obviously connected and often intertwined. To put it simply, full-time Reverend Jones holds an identity as Reverend Jones and if he, for example, happens to be a parent or belongs to certain organizations centered on a particular interest, he may be seen by others in those roles, yet the primary way by which his professional identity is known is through his role as minister.

Contrast this with my situation. As a public school counselor for twenty-one years, I have served in schools in the town in which I live, where more than seventeen hundred students attend, thirty minutes away from the church in which I serve. Were you to walk into my public school office, you would not see anything indicating to you that I happened to be an ordained clergyman. My students have known me as Mr. LaRochelle, at least until I obtained the advanced degree that switched my title over to Dr. LaRochelle. I provide counseling services, including postsecondary guidance, for individuals of a wide variety of religious persuasions, including none at all. Friends of mine among my colleagues know that I am a minister because they happen to know me and my family pretty well and many of them also happened to be present at my ordination a few years back. My suspicion is that the majority of my students have no idea that I am ordained and serve a church as a pastor and that a very large number of faculty are unaware as well. This lack of awareness is not because I am trying to hide anything, because I am not, yet rather because my role in the school is to serve as a member of the school Counseling Department, and I will both respond to people and be evaluated within the parameters of that role. In addition, as a public school employee who holds to a firm belief in the separation of church and state, I am opposed to any behavior on my part that could be construed or interpreted as proselytizing or evangelizing in any way, shape, or form.

Where it all gets interesting and unique is when those persons, often students, but usually fellow employees, who have known me in my working role, either discover that I am a minister or in their interactions with me become highly cognizant of the fact that, to put it in the vernacular, "Oh, My God, I'm talking to a 'man of the cloth.'" (I've heard that one more than a few times!) My experience has been that when office conversation turns to something that may include a sexual reference or joke or some other "worldly" matter, people hesitate to continue the conversation around me, often giving the impression that it is inappropriate to talk about certain things, especially sex, around this "man of the cloth." The bivocational minister, on his or her "day job," will most likely run into this experience, what I call a perceived otherness, that is, a sense on the part of a colleague that there is something different about this person called minister.

This, I think, is all symptomatic of a greater reality that is evidenced in the world of full-time ministers as well. Most people really simply do not understand what it is like to be a clergyman or clergywoman, and so they see those who choose those professions as sort of out of the mainstream. I don't say this as criticism. I simply state it as something I observe. The profession of ministry is just seen differently from other jobs. People may not understand what it's like to be an auto mechanic or accountant or teacher or doctor, but most of us understand that if you are trained in those fields, those are jobs that you do. But ministry involves this institution called a church, and as a minister, priest, or rabbi, you've got to get up and talk about God, sometimes when standing in front of coffins at funerals. There's just something strangely different about this job in the eyes of so many.

Much of this has to do with the way people perceived clergy if they grew up within a religious institution. Even if they have long since broken away from the church of their youth, their understanding of pastor might come from that priest or minister whom they knew as a kid. This past experience influences how they perceive their coworker who happens not only to work with them but who is one of those "religious people" too.

For many other coworkers, as for a large number who look at the position of full-time pastor out in their own hometowns, the world of the church is really foreign territory. The overwhelming majority of Americans do not attend church services on a regular basis. Consequently most people do not have regular interactions with clergy. Even within many churches, the priest or minister is someone whom you see "up there" once a week or less, someone with whom you have little interaction outside of that limited block of time.

For most Americans today, the minister is someone who might appear at some of the weddings you might attend or who conducts the prayers at a memorial service or at someone's grave. Most people see their dentist or gynecologist or gastrointestinal specialist more in the course of a decade than they see a "man (or woman) of the cloth," so to speak.

Herein lies the fascinating location of the bivocational minister in the overall ministry of the universal Christian church. The bivocational minister employed in a secular job that has nothing to do with call or ordination (such as my work as a school counselor) is in the unique position of being a representative of the church in a context outside of the traditional church setting. Through this unique means, the minister embodies the values of Christianity beyond the walls of the church. In the most ideal sense, the minister not only represents the church in the everyday "real world" but also is able to bring a real-world perspective to the deliberations and decision-making processes of the local church.

There are some elements of danger in the notion that a clergyperson "represents" the church in his or her worldly job. If we take seriously the mission of all Christian believers, then we recognize that all who believe in Christ carry their Christianity to whatever circumstances in which they find themselves. The nonordained engineer, nurse, and custodian who believe in Jesus and are a part of the church bring the faith of the church into their offices and other workplaces through their very persons. This is the essence of the belief in a "priesthood of all believers" expressed in Martin Luther's maxim "Every person a priest, and every person a priest to every other person."[1]

Nonetheless, one can hold firmly to this conviction of a shared priesthood of the ordained and laity and still recognize that, by dint of chosen profession, a clergyman or clergywoman does serve as visible representative of his or her other particular community of faith and by training and skill is equipped to represent that faith in a variety of settings. Thus the bivocational minister who holds a secular job finds himself or herself in a somewhat unique position. If the experience of other ministers in this situation is like my own, over the course of time that minister in the secular office will be pulled aside and asked all kinds of questions about God and church policy. She or he will hear stories about past interactions with clergy and churches and of hurts that will not go away. He or she will be invited to perform weddings, offer pastoral care to family members, and advise on a wide variety of topics. It will not be unusual for the minister who is well respected personally to be entrusted with a coworker's secrets, including those matters that might be deemed confessional and penitential in nature. He or she might also become a resource in helping to resolve conflict within the institution in which the minister happens to work.

Sometimes things happen serendipitously as well. Recently I received a call from the mother of a young man I worked with when I was his guidance counselor in middle school quite a long time ago. While this mom did not really know with which church I was affiliated, she had heard that I did something official in my church. When this former student died tragically at a young age while living hundreds of miles away and the family decided to hold his funeral back in Connecticut where he grew up, she asked me to speak at his funeral service. It was a real opportunity for ministerial outreach and a time to witness to the hope of the gospel that occurred as a result of my secular profession as a public school employee.

If a bivocational pastor listens well and asks the right questions, working side by side with others can give the pastor amazing insights into what might constitute good worship and preaching as well as regarding what the church might be able to do to respond well in the lives of those who consider it irrelevant. I have learned a lot about preaching from asking the opinions of coworkers who have sat in the pews of churches other than my own. Through them, I have learned much not only about what I should do, but also about what I had better be sure that I don't do. As an individual who works a full week and has responsibilities that can be quite exhausting, I have also gained insight into what it must be like to volunteer to be on a church board or committee or devote time to singing in the choir or making sandwiches for the soup kitchen. I think that, as a result of my working in the "real" world, I have developed empathy for those in the church who come to meetings and are impatient if too much time is taken up talking about things with limited productivity as a result. As a bivocational minister, I have also been fortunate to be able to bring insights and research from another professional field into the work of church ministry.

Someone reading this may think that my enthusiasm for bivocational ministry carries with it the implication that there is something deficient in the full-time model. I don't want to convey that impression. As a matter of fact, before I retire, if I ever do, I hope to have the experience of working full-time in the area of professional ministry. The simple reality is that every approach to job structuring contains both strengths and drawbacks. From my observations, the full-time pastor must of necessity channel his or her energy into the ministry of the church. While others in the congregation are at their offices and assembly lines during the day, the full-time pastor is often on site at the church building conjuring up strategies for those evening board and committee meetings to which many of the congregants will stumble in after a full day's work, with or without benefit of touching base at home and maybe even eating dinner.

The congregation will most certainly benefit from the pastor who has had the opportunity to engage in detailed systematic analysis of the church's issues. Yet, on some level, the full-time pastor, for whom the work of the church is a central focus of professional life, can sometimes hold subtly to an expectation that it will hold that place of prominence in the work life of those board and committee members as well. The bivocational pastor would most likely have a higher comfort level with the strains and demands of those people sitting on church council or on the board of trustees, knowing firsthand that he or she is juggling this commitment to the church with a full bevy of outside work obligations, all while attempting to place primary focus on one's relational life with others and ultimately with that ground of being and reality to which we give the name God. One could counter by saying that the church with the bivocational pastor loses out in that it has no one whose primary focus is the systematic reflection the church needs. These are the kinds of issues and questions churches, search committees, and candidates need to lay on the table as they discuss the viability of a bivocational model in their congregations.

Much insight into bivocational ministry has come from the lived experience of the permanent diaconate in the Roman Catholic Church. Many people within Protestant communities, including denominational officials, seem to have a limited understanding of this ministry within the life of the Catholic Church and its applicability to the issue of part-time pastoring. Thus it is important that we review some of the important facts regarding this ministerial model.[2]

Since the end of the Second Vatican Council in the mid 1960s, the Catholic Church in America has ordained a large number of permanent deacons. The council itself called for "the restoration of the permanent diaconate" in the life of the church. In this country, the increase in ordained deacons has served to fill a void caused by a significant decrease in the number of priests being ordained within Catholicism. It has been well noted that ordination to the priesthood is usually restricted to unmarried men who are expected to live a celibate life and is not open to women at all.

In the Roman Catholic understanding of ministry, the deacon is an ordained clergyman who has received the Sacrament of Holy Orders, a sacrament that contains three ministries within it: deacon, priest (presbyter), and bishop. Under the authority of the bishop, the permanent deacon (permanent because in the Sacrament of Holy Orders, one is configured to the ministry of the church for life) is able to perform certain public functions as an official representative of the church: He may conduct wedding ceremonies, perform baptisms, preach at mass and other services, conduct Benediction of the Blessed Sacrament, administer blessings, officiate at wake services and funerals, bless sacramentals (such as ashes for use on Ash Wednesday), grant some dispensations to lay Catholics, and preside at communion services where a priest is not present. Certain actions for which a bishop or priest is ordained may not be performed by a permanent deacon: He may not preside at mass or consecrate the eucharist. He may not hear confessions or administer absolution. He may not administer the sacrament of Anointing of the Sick, though he may lead prayers at the bedside of the dying and give Viaticum (communion for the journey from death to eternal life).

Especially because massive reductions in the priesthood have forced local Catholic dioceses to often assign priests to serve as pastors to two or more parishes at a time, permanent deacons have served a needed function of providing many services within Catholic parishes. While a number of permanent deacons come from the ranks of the retired, the majority are men who hold a full-time job and are ordinarily married and have children.

I do have theological difficulties with how the diaconate is defined and am troubled by Catholicism's position on celibacy for priests and denying the priesthood to women. In fact, these issues were part of the confluence of factors that led me to resign from the diaconate. (Though how does one resign from that which is permanent? Perhaps I'll deal with that issue someday in another book or article.) However, I do believe that Protestantism can learn from the considerable body of work that has been developed for permanent deacons and those institutions in which they serve. Catholic permanent deacons have been in the forefront of dealing with the specific and concrete issues regarding representative presence in the world as an ordained minister in the church as well as bringing the needs of those in the marketplace into the arena of discussion within the church. Likewise, on an individual basis, permanent deacons have had to deal with the time management and organizational issues bivocational, part-time pastors must confront in their parish work.

Again I draw from my own experience. My ministry as a Catholic permanent deacon was a wonderful training ground for what I do now as a part-time pastor in a congregation of the United Church of Christ. I was ordained a permanent deacon in the Archdiocese of Hartford, assigned by the archbishop to the pastoral staff of a local Roman Catholic parish. In this capacity, over a nine-year period, I preached four masses each weekend on a regular basis; conducted Ash Wednesday services, Stations of the Cross, and Benediction of the Blessed Sacrament regularly; conducted public worship services of our local parish; ran the Rite of Christian Initiation of Adults (RCIA); conducted the baptismal preparation for the parish; baptized more than 250 individuals; performed nearly fifty weddings; presided at numerous wakes and funerals; counseled engaged couples; assisted divorced individuals with annulment petitions; visited hospitals and nursing homes; and worked with children and youth—all in addition to holding a full-time job in the local school system.

For a period of nearly two years, the pastor and I were the only two individuals on the staff of this parish, a congregation that serviced more than seven thousand individuals in the town in which it was located. As a result, I preached at all of the masses every other weekend and increased the time spent on each of the services I described above. There is no question that I and the large number of Catholic permanent deacons engaged in ministry throughout this country and the world can offer living insights to those who seek to consider a bivocational path.

While recognizing theological differences over the place of ordination, the historic differences between the churches, and the reality that the role of pastor does carry within it some differences from the role of deacon as ordinarily defined, I remain convinced that those charged with training local pastors in Protestant denominations should draw from the considerable resources available to the wider church from the Roman Catholic permanent diaconate. I would also encourage seminarians and ordained ministers reading this text to explore the bibliographical resources I provide in this book. In addition, search committees and placement officers may find in these materials some inspiration as they seek to identify significant questions to explore in considering the applicability of a bivocational ministry within a particular congregation. I encourage those who turn to these resources not to let theological or denominational differences serve as impediments to a helpful understanding.

It is my firm conviction, based both upon theological reflection and lived experience, that the bivocational pastor can bring a unique perspective to the local congregation and can serve as a helpful pastoral presence within those institutions in which he or she lives out one's secular employment. With due respect to those of a more conservative, evangelical approach, I caution that the workplace should not become the arena for trying to convert or "save" one's fellow workers. The primary responsibility of working in the workplace is to do the job that is required there. In fact, the minister in this situation has to work through various scenarios in which his or her pastoral inclination and the responsibilities of the job may be in tension.

As a public school employee, I face this tension all the time. Here I will cite but one example, one that occurs over and over again in many different presentations and incarnations. In working with young people, dealing with their families, and hearing their stories of emotional ups and downs, there are many times when I find myself thinking that some of these students in front of me have a spiritual void in their lives, that they would benefit from an in-depth consideration of whether a relationship with God might benefit their lives, and that they could really use the opportunity to read the New Testament as well as other valuable Christian resources and get to know something about Jesus, his values, and his teachings. Yet, as a public school employee, as someone who should not be promoting established religion, I cannot and I will not suggest to them that they do so. I will ask questions of them regarding outside relationships or people who influence them and to whom they might confide—rabbi, priest, minister, scout leader, swim coach, or the like. But I will not suggest that they start going to church, temple, retreat, or their local youth group, however much I feel it might benefit them. Conversely, as a mainline Christian who values biblical scholarship, reason, interfaith dialogue, and an inclusive Christian vision, there are times when I feel that the religious perspective espoused by some students and explained by them to me in my office is really bad Christian theology and unhealthy religion. I may think this, but in fulfilling my role as a public school counselor, I cannot in any way convey that to them, as much as it may kill me, as much as I'd like to say, "Get out of that way of thinking now, before it completely eats you up. Discard that theology before you throw God out somewhere down the road."

So, yes, there can be tension in bivocational ministry, but it's the real-life tension of helping God's people wherever they may be in God's very real, everyday world! It's an exciting and wonderfully rewarding ministry indeed!

Discussion Questions:

1. Evaluate the author's comments on the Roman Catholic Permanent Diaconate in terms of understanding bivocational ministry.

2. Please comment on the author's observations about the bivocational minister in the workplace.

5

Understanding the Small Church

The bivocational or part-time pastor is usually employed by those churches that are considered to be "small." In the last several decades there has been a considerable, helpful body of literature about small churches. While it is not my purpose to repeat all of it here, it is useful to review some pertinent information when considering alternative approaches to ministry. Over these next few pages, I will make observations from the available literature and refer specifically to my own experience as a small church bivocational pastor.

Each congregation, regardless of its size, is a unique entity with its own particular history, customs, traditions, and means of operation. Yet small churches do function quite differently from their larger counterparts—a reality explored in considerable detail in the extensive body of literature that has developed in recent years. One could say that there is a clear relationship between church size and identity. The literature provides both characterizations and definitions of the various types of churches based upon church size. For example, Roy Oswald, among others, notes that a significant feature of the small church is a sense of "family."[1] It is not uncommon to find the terms "small church" and "family church" used interchangeably.

What is often called the small or pastoral church most readily has some sense of self-identification as "family," with whatever that term might imply. This is certainly an apt description of the Congregational Church of Union, United Church of Christ. When I was called to serve the church as pastor in 2001, average church attendance was twenty-nine. Closer examination found church members from among the same several families, including individuals who had held positions of leadership for a number of years. Highly intriguing to me is the identity of a small church that exists within a small town, as a small community within a small community—a civic community, in fact, that uses the language of family to describe itself as a local town. Much has been written about the dynamics and the features of small towns in America. While recognizing inherent varieties of small towns, dependent upon geographic location, economic factors, and so on, it is clear that small communities function differently from larger ones. Thus the art and reality of pastoring small churches must distinguish among types of small churches that exist out there in the land of American small church religion:

- ⚭ Small community churches like mine in America's small towns, many of which were once much larger than they are today.

- ⚭ Long-standing established churches often found in larger cities, churches that were once considered large or medium-sized, many of whose congregants have moved away from the old neighborhood. These churches often have very limited attendance in rather large space.

↝ New church starts that many denominations are now seeking to foster.

Any local church trying to identify what it is seeking in a new pastor must first be able to articulate for its search committee how it envisions itself as a small church. When I was called to be pastor at my church in Union, Connecticut, I sought to read as much as I could about small churches and small towns, which proved to be most helpful in learning about potential dynamics within our congregation. Yet, early on in my pastorate, yet another reality began to sink in. Not only is our church a very small church in the smallest community in the relatively small state of Connecticut, it is also the only Christian church of any denomination in the town of Union. In addition, it is the only organized congregation of any religious tradition in the town. This fact is not insignificant! Early on in my pastoral tenure, I discovered several valuable historical documents that detailed the establishment and development of our congregation and offered insights into the uniqueness of our situation. This quote from our most extensive piece of historical writing is quite revealing:

> In the final analysis both the church and the town are characterized by simple friendship and caring, qualities difficult to come by in these times. These are gifts to be cherished and preserved. The church that started a town has survived for 250 years, despite adversity, impossible odds, through low membership, lack of ministry, and extreme poverty. It has survived primarily because of the strong faith and sound character of its membership and townsmen.[2]

This quotation indicates both the strong sense and the heritage of survival, for as the author notes in many places, the congregation endured many difficult financial times and lengthy periods when the church was without a pastor and services were rarely conducted. Likewise, this passage recognizes what is quite clear throughout the church's history: that the church is valued as a significant institution within this community, an institution fully enmeshed in Union's formation and continuation.

On a personal level, I had been advised that as Union's minister I would really be the town chaplain and could well expect to be called upon by townspeople both for counsel and the performance of rituals commonly associated with clergy. I was fascinated with the fact that the church newsletter was also the town newsletter, whose mailing list included all current residents and those former ones who wished to stay connected to their old hometown. As a result, it is not unusual for people in Union who rarely attend church services to associate with this church and call it theirs, for, in a very concrete and real sense, it is the town church.

I became fascinated with the history of the church and the relationship between church and town. Our church sits across from the town green in the heart of this New England community, which dates back to 1734. The church itself was established on December 13, 1738. The church's spacious Parish Hall is the center for town and school social functions and church dinners and musical performances. These social activities sponsored by the church regularly attract residents of the community who do not participate in the church's worship.

In a longstanding town tradition, the local pastor is expected to take an active part in a very unique Memorial Day celebration in which town members, rather than just watching the parade, in fact are the parade, all those able bodied actually marching along in it! The community holds an Annual "Old Home Day" celebration on the third Saturday in August, the foundation of which was rooted in the life and program of the church and in which the congregation is actively engaged up to this day. The church's annual Christmas pageant is one of the most heavily attended local events of any calendar year. Our church has recently instituted several initiatives to provide social and communitarian opportunities for residents of the town, including highly successful concerts, dinners, and a richly appreciated Holly Day (Christmas) Fair.

Throughout my first year as a new pastor, I was privileged to be under the mentorship of an experienced local pastor, the chair of our association's committee on ministry. As I met with him monthly and reflected upon my new call, I became ever more deeply struck by the reality that our church was the only community of any Christian tradition within the town. I began to wonder aloud about how church members perceived the differences, if any, between the institution of the church and the other strong institutions within this historic place.

Such questions necessarily brought me back to my own ecclesiological foundations and to those issues regarding how I perceived the institutional church. As my early days as pastor in Union moved along, my initial sense that I would enjoy my ministry was reinforced and deepened. People were kind, generous, supportive, and loving, very positive about the sermons that I preached and about the work that I was doing. Despite the fact that we were small, the growing multigenerational blend within our congregation and the fact that new people in town were visiting our church and coming back to stay were both very exciting to me. In a two-year period, our weekly attendance rose from twenty-nine to forty-four people, an active youth ministry program was formed, and the church's tremendous spirit of volunteerism flourished. People responded extremely well to requests for mission projects, and our music program thrived and prospered as one of our organists offered new and exciting opportunities for people of all ages to get involved. As individuals grew in their trust of me, I, in turn, felt quite comfortable preaching with more frequency on so-called "controversial" topics. I was pleased that many individuals took advantage of the opportunities for dialogue that I was offering and were willing to disagree with some of my conclusions, even as they were personally both kind and affirming.

During this period, prior to beginning my doctoral work, I found myself emphasizing certain themes in my preaching, primary among them the concept of welcoming, as expressive of a biblically based hospitality within the context of contemporary life. In retrospect, I see that I was reacting to what I saw as one of our congregation's strengths, this sense of kindness and neighborly hospitality. This is what my family and I felt as we were ourselves welcomed into this community, even though we were (and are) residents of a suburb of Hartford nearly thirty miles away, even though I am a former Roman Catholic clergyperson and part-time bivocational pastor and my wife and children all currently remain Roman Catholics. Quite honestly, I was most encouraged by how our congregation embraced some of the innovations in worship I introduced as well as much of the new music I invited them to sing, all of which led to a very trusting decision to purchase a new hymnal. I soon learned that one of my favorite hymns, quite new to this congregation—Marty Haugen's "All Are Welcome"—was becoming something of a motto and a reference point for people in the church.[3] People told me that they enjoyed the song and that it captured what they felt in some way about who we are. The phrase, "All Are Welcome," which I had started to put into the bulletin and newsletter on a regular basis, was showing up in our conversations and deliberations in various meetings of committees and boards within our church. In looking back, I understand that this initial period of reflection as I assumed a new call, this time of discernment, contained within itself the core of what I would come to develop as a set of beliefs concerning the development of church identity within the specific context of this marvelous small town.

As many of these initiatives were unfolding and as I was beginning to venture out even more and preach extensively on such controversial issues as the abolition of the death penalty and the United Church of Christ's marriage equality resolution, I became deeply immersed in my doctoral studies in the Association of Chicago Theological Schools' Doctor of Ministry in Preaching program. I began to understand more completely the role that preaching plays in both developing and articulating a church's identity, giving voice to the hopes, dreams, and visions that emerge from the life of a congregation.[4]

As a result of my study, rooted in the specific history and heritage of my own church, I remain convinced that the small church pastor, bivocational, part-time, or not, must engage in the ongoing process of dialogue about that particular congregation's identity. This articulation of identity must be front and center and on the table in all of the discussions that lead to the call of a new pastor. One of the fundamental questions search committees and pastoral candidates must face in the search and call process is that of the relationship between the part-time nature of the position and the church's ability to deepen and live out its desired identity. I strongly believe that the pastor, through the process of preaching and the ongoing dialogue that both flows from and leads back to the pastor's preaching, must immerse herself or himself in the congregation's process of engaging in this task. The pastor or church who calls the pastor to provide little more than weekly supply preaching and emergency pastoral services simply cannot fulfill this facet of church mission. Rather, the part-time pastor must be front and center in this process, as identity formation and living is so integral to the work of any church.

I reiterate that each local church has to come to terms with its own identity, one that may very well evolve and develop over the course of a congregation's life. In our congregation's case, our own development has been rooted in the heritage of the congregation, as understood through a studied evaluation of our history. From its beginnings, there was a strong relationship between the church and community in Union and a sense that even those who were not formally members of the church saw themselves as, in some way, connected to it. Those small town qualities of friendliness and hospitality that marked the history of the town were also reflected in the work of the church over the years. In a sense, the congregation's twenty-first-century decision first to allow same-sex civil unions in its sanctuary and then marriage between homosexuals when Connecticut's law changed is rooted in some strains of thinking and conviction that have been present throughout the church's history, while definitely appropriated to the changing circumstances of the contemporary context.

Other congregations operate out of different histories. I think of a church here in Connecticut, once a prominent mainline Protestant mid-city church, now housing very few worshipers on a weekly basis, yet maintaining an amazing inner city ministry to the homeless population in a local community in which homelessness is deep-seated and pervasive. The current actions of that small church in this changed cultural context is in keeping with the church's long-standing heritage of being an active force within that Connecticut town.

Available data shows that the majority of churches in this country are identified as small ones. These small churches come in different shapes and forms, yet they contain a great capacity for proclamation of the gospel of Jesus Christ in a way appropriate to the emerging needs of the communities of which they are a part. They also carry great potential to be progressive and alive, for their strength lies in the qualities of relationships between and among their members and with a sense of mutual solidarity and familial caring so desperately needed in an all too impersonal modern world.

The bivocational pastor, despite the considerable demands of her or his other vocation, is vitally needed to be a key active part of the ongoing conversation of the small church she or he is called to serve. To maximize one's ministerial strength within a congregation, one has to commit oneself to a study of its history and heritage, its values and goals, its hopes and its dreams. Exciting work indeed! Necessary work for the future of the church of Jesus Christ!

Discussion Questions: *Keep defining identity...*

1. Evaluate the author's view of the small church.

2. Comment on what the author says about the centrality of identifying a church's identity. What is your experience of this in the churches of which you have been a part?

6

Concrete Suggestions for Churches and Pastors

I begin this chapter by posing a doomsday scenario. Disastrous, unintended negative effects might very well arise should a church do a poor job in selecting a part-time or bivocational pastor. A choice that is not well thought out and whose implications are not fully considered and worked out can lead to frustration, disillusionment, and negativity in the local congregation, thereby thwarting the mission of the church, leading to decline in both energy and attendance, and perhaps even calling the congregation's ability to function in the future into question. Now, how's that for doom and gloom?

All kidding aside, there is a great deal of truth in such a scenario. Search committees are composed of busy people, often with their own full-time worries and needs. When a pastoral vacancy occurs in their church, it is natural that they will want to fill it as quickly as possible to insure that the congregation will benefit from the necessary services of a clergyperson and that someone will be readily available to provide a continuity of preaching and the requisite pastoral care.

In filling pastoral vacancies, congregations that, through their polity, have the authority to hire a minister, are to a great extent dependent upon the resources of the denomination to guide them in their search. Many denominations, including my own, the United Church of Christ, have highly developed procedures for engaging the whole church in formulating a profile, in helping the congregation acquire the services of a qualified interim minister, and in assisting church membership in understanding that the interim period carries with it some vital tasks. I have found that many, if not most, congregations do these tasks well. Yet, more than occasionally, one hears something else. You might hear rumblings from the congregation as to whether the search committee ever really researched how well this guy could preach or you might hear people ask if anyone ever knew that she, the new pastor, was really as aloof as she has presented herself. Or in private moments you might hear pastors confiding to their colleagues that they feel they might have been misled a bit by the search committees with whom they worked, that the congregation really wanted someone with a different set of skills than those highlighted throughout this pastoral search process.

It is my sense that these afterthoughts are exacerbated by the particular uniqueness and interpretive range involved in the calling of a part-time pastor, especially one who might simultaneously be employed elsewhere. Situations may arise during the course of the individual's pastorate, often fairly early on after that honeymoon period (if there is one) that cause rumblings to start through the congregation:

- Did you hear that our new minister hasn't visited Mrs. Smith yet? Can you believe that?

- Looks like he doesn't really care about spending time with our youth.

- Sometimes I wonder if she spends much time preparing her sermons. They all seem so rushed.

- Do you ever notice how quickly he tries to leave at coffee hour and how he really doesn't spend that much time around the church?

- I wish our minister did what that other church's minister does. Did you ever notice how she shows up at school events and local Little League games and things like that?

- I've noticed that our new minister tries to wiggle out of as much meeting time as he possibly can!

- I don't see where our new pastor is giving us any new ideas!

- Doesn't look good. He's been here three months and attendance is the same. I don't think we are going to take in much more money either!

- I think we might have made a mistake hiring this one!

The usual process of calling a new minister is stressful in and of itself. It is even tougher when you are looking for someone part-time. Toughest of all is when you are "scaling down" from having someone on the job full-time, that very fact being in a real sense connected to the church's identity as a presence within the community. Denominations in which search committees are not quite so active and that rely on placement officers and denominational officials need to be deeply attentive to all of these issues as well.

THE INTERIM PERIOD

There are two glaring ways that congregations and/or those involved with them really fail in doing justice to the search process. The first and more obvious is an inadequate and incomplete articulation and dialogue within the church, within the candidate him- or herself, and between the candidate and the church's representative. The second goes against the conventional wisdom and practice of many denominations in the local setting. It has to do with the length of the interim period and how, unintentionally, a church may preclude the necessary exploration of possible pastoral candidates and may even unnecessarily render good candidates unavailable.

Thus in this chapter I suggest ways to be well prepared as a candidate or as someone responsible for hiring a part-time pastor, ways to engage in a process that will lead to a good decision. I offer some very practical questions you can ask each other and explain the enormous role the entire church must play in this process. But first, let me explain why I think the interim period has potential to be counterproductive and in some cases contributes to undesired results.

First, let's clarify—outstanding work has been done in the area of training interim ministers and in helping congregations understand the uniqueness of the interim tasks.[1] Second, some congregations will benefit from fairly long-term interim pastorates because of the particular circumstances that have led to the pastoral vacancy. My direct immersion in the work of the United Church of Christ came through a period in which I served as a director of Christian education during the time of an interim pastorate. In that particular case, the congregation was reeling from the suicide of its long-term and highly respected pastor on the Monday of Holy Week, all compounded by allegations of sexual misconduct directed at him. I learned through my work with children and youth that he had been held in much esteem by the younger members of this congregation, and this entire chapter in the life of a wonderful congregation was indescribably painful.

This interim situation is markedly different from another in a community just a few miles away in which a distinguished local pastor retired of his own volition after a wonderful, noteworthy career. In the first situation, there was raw emotional intensity in the congregation—an air of toxicity in which a climate of blaming and rationalizing created an ongoing sense of internal war. In the latter situation, a congregation was left in really good shape, ready for a new minister to come and build upon the longstanding good that had been done.

So what is the length of time needed to conduct an appropriate search for what is known as a "settled pastor" (interesting term!)? Those who specialize in the area of interim ministry stress that congregations not rush through the process and be very deliberate about identifying interim tasks. In a similar vein, congregations need to take this time to identify their goals and how these goals might relate to the background and skills they expect in a settled pastor. A lack of due deliberation can lead to difficult circumstances down the road for both pastor and congregation.

It would be a mistake to assume that the more difficult the cause of the pastoral vacancy the longer the interim period should be. The church that had to deal with its pastor's suicide, and some of the issues surrounding it, quite obviously had a lot to work out. Any temptation to "put the past behind and move on" without due regard for a complete and thorough review of the climate of the congregation would be most problematic. Yet in the other church, blessed by a good, healthy relationship over time, there could be a difficult issue as well: How does one follow someone so beloved? How does a congregation deal with the fact that there will be inevitable comparisons between the former, beloved pastor and the new man or woman? All of this would get even more complicated if the new person moved into a pastoral situation in which the church had decided to scale back to something more part-time. It is therefore hard to argue with the wisdom that a local congregation should not rush through this process.

Having said this, I encourage readers to consider another angle. In my discussions with members of search committees in small churches, I have heard some rumblings of concern that denominational officials tend to influence congregations toward a slower *why grumble -?*

search process than necessary. I have also heard concerns expressed that potential pastoral candidates, individuals whose leadership might really benefit particular churches, become unavailable to these churches because of the way this process is handled.

The time frame concern is certainly legitimate, though I also would not place the blame on denominational officials. The reality is that when a minister is ready to seek out either a first call or a new congregation, he or she is operating within a time frame greatly determined by personal and/or family considerations at that time. He or she might know of a particular church that has a pastoral opening, a church of high interest to the individual, yet in the time it takes for the actual position to be posted, for profiles to be read and interviews to be conducted, the candidate might end up looking at and even taking a call at another church.

Parenthetically, local congregations led by interim pastors often tend to experience a drop-off in attendance during the interim period and a diminution of potential for new members because interested individuals prefer to wait to see which direction the congregation will move under the settled pastor. When I decided to leave the Catholic Church, such was my own experience in a congregation of a denomination that had some appeal to me. I was attending worship at the local church, the one with which I most likely would have affiliated, and I sensed a congregation in flux, just waiting to see what was going to happen next. My motivation to wait with them conflicted with my desire to make some important decisions regarding church affiliation, and I did not really consider that congregation seriously from that point on.

I admire denominational officials for many of the processes that have been developed by church leadership to assist congregations in the search and call process. The United Church of Christ's *Manual on Ministry*[2] is an outstanding resource to assist congregational leadership in navigating through this process. But I wish to challenge both search committees and the denominational leaders who work with them to look at better ways of moving the process along.

In a recent conversation with some search committee members in a really exciting small local church, a church with a marvelous heritage and great potential for its future, I asked why the church was moving into its fourth year in an interim period. In fact, they have just called their second interim pastor. My conversation with one of the members indicated that the local denominational conference had instituted a new program for churches in their situation but that this new program had not completely gotten off the ground. Quite frankly, I can't help but think that in this three-plus year period, this church, one with marvelous internal resources, may have missed out on getting a very good pastor and, in turn, the church's potential outreach to its community was considerably diminished during that time.

This is hardly an isolated case. If anything, with the proliferation of small churches seeking part-time ministers, I am starting to see this happen more and more. In some scenarios, local churches end up having difficulty providing enough supply preachers to meet the needs of their worshiping community or resort to a rotating supply system that, while providing variety and diversity of preaching and worship styles, tends to do very little to provide for thematic continuity over the course of a liturgical year. *important*

I'm willing to concede that committees take their cue from denominational officials, who tend to highlight the importance of this interim period. Congregations seeking new pastors are in somewhat of a vulnerable position and trust these officials to guide them through a wilderness of uncertainty . . . and paperwork! Yet, ultimately, it is my sense that local committees need to recognize that there are built-in factors on the local level that serve as impediments to the process and they need to find creative ways to remove those impediments and thus streamline their search without sacrificing its quality.

SEARCH COMMITTEES AND EFFICIENCY

Let's talk specifics: The typical church search committee is composed of volunteers, often very busy individuals. These are people with jobs that may very well demand evening hours or travel. Scheduling common meeting time can be difficult. Committee members may have their schedules influenced to a great extent by school vacations or built-in breaks during the year in which people concede that not much will happen (such as holidays) and that it is best to resume serious searching when more people will be around. I know of one church whose search essentially came to a halt for two consecutive summers. It seems to me that these built-in impediments may very well hurt the overall process and exclude potential candidates along the way. Again, I think this can get even more complicated when part-time ministry, including considerations of structuring hours and salary, are factored into the mix. A committee can even be lulled into complacency when the interim pastor is doing a good job. They learn to rely on him or her. They may even really like this new minister and would like to keep this person around for as long as possible. Church insiders might be quite susceptible to this phenomenon because it considerably diminishes their sense of urgency. It might even work out well for the interim minister, who is not faced with having to go out and find a new position all that quickly and instead can have some job security for awhile!

These impediments and obstacles can be dealt with head on through approaches and methodologies that work for the local congregation. Now, what works for your church may not work for mine. But, in all cases, the congregation should be willing to think creatively as it structures its meeting times and the responsibilities of committee members between meetings.

First, let's examine the usual structuring of the search process: A committee settles a time with a denominational official and discusses the process before proceeding to meet together to engage in the painstaking task of creating a profile, with input from the different boards and committees of the church and with appropriate survey construction and data from the congregation. This often takes quite a while. The committee usually schedules regular meetings, weekly in some congregations, less so in others, in which all members are updated on the progress. This meeting schedule is often staggered as a result of vacation breaks, often scheduled around school and summer.

At some point, the local church is ready to advertise that it is looking for a minister and then begins a new painstaking process: reading profiles, resumes, curricula vitae, and the like. From that point, they proceed to decide whom to interview, how to interview (which often includes a session being coached in proper interviewing techniques, often by a denominational official), what kind of questions to construct for an interview, and whether to gather more information on prospective candidates. They ask themselves whether members should go and hear candidates preach, how many candidates to see, and how many committee members should go. If they decide to requisition videotaped sermons from prospective candidates, they may have difficulty working out a streamlined process for committee members to adequately review this videotaped material.

All of this is simply a thumbnail sketch of the far more complicated work of this group of volunteers, people with lives beyond the church, who constitute this often mysterious entity within the congregation known as the search committee. Is it not possible that these enormous tasks can be accomplished in a more timely fashion so that the congregation does not miss out on important pastoral opportunities yet without sacrificing the integrity and necessity of the search process or the interim period or both? Is it not also possible that committees can find ways to use this time more efficiently when they are confronted by the complexities caused by a consideration of a part-time, maybe even potentially bivocational minister?

Some may contend that the current system allows those involved in the search process to be fully immersed in and take ownership of it. I'm not so certain. I once asked a search committee about the reasons for the previous pastor's departure from the church, a fact that was stated within the profile they had provided for me. After I quoted from the profile, a committee member turned to the entire group and asked, "Did we write that in there?" obviously not knowing that they had. Of course, in all of our jobs and tasks, we are bombarded with information and may forget some specifics of certain things sometimes. I have a knack for forgetting to bring laundry up and change light bulbs, for sure! But it seems to me that if an entire committee has been working on a pastoral vacancy for a while and has gone through the task of creating a representative profile, all of its members are going to have a good handle regarding what is in it unless, of course, the search period has been so protracted that people are too far removed from what they originally wrote! This is to say that creative restructuring of a committee's time may not detract from the quality of the finished product. It may even strengthen it!

Certain procedural adjustments that may prove helpful include the following:

- Maximize the use of technology among committee and church members to provide for the best and most efficient collection of necessary data as soon as possible. Hold to time limits, including clearly delineated time frames to collect data, whether from those who share it technologically or from congregants uninterested in using these means. Explore different methodologies whereby search committee members can conference with each other about assigned tasks, perhaps using a Facebook page or Twitter accounts or some creative use of the church's website. I suspect that there is expertise within most congregations; if not, the denomination probably has technological consultants.

- Rethink the timeline and structure of meeting times. Are the frequency and time period scheduled for these meetings effectively moving this process along? Explore the viability of weekend morning retreats on two or three tasks of the search process, assigning profiles to subgroups within the larger committee and increasing report-backs and summarizations so that the entire committee is freed from poring over every piece of paper that comes in. This will cut duplication costs as well.

- Do not let time go by where the process is put on hold. Even when few people are around (such as the July 4 vacation period), assign tasks to individuals, which keeps the process moving forward. I have seen pastoral searches grind to a screeching halt during certain periods of time. Those time blocks can add up quickly, which can hinder a congregation's efforts to get the best possible pastoral leadership available.

- Be sure to consult with the local denominational official to find out who is available or looking for a church who may be of interest to this congregation based on the needs that have been expressed.

- Consider bringing in trusted pastors from your or other denominations to review congregational issues with you and to give you consultative feedback about your congregation.

These are just a few practical suggestions. More will likely emerge from the sharing of the lived unique experience of your congregation. A few more suggestions:

1. Think creatively. Do not be limited by some set search committee model.

2. Use consultative services both within and outside your denomination.

3. Challenge the effectiveness of meetings and be willing to adjust your meeting calendar accordingly.

4. Move large group tasks more frequently to smaller groups with report-back responsibilities.

5. Consider how technology can increase efficiency.

6. Tap the potential of one another in the room.

7. Without violating confidentiality, engage your congregation as often as possible. All too often, a sense of mystery enshrouds search committees to the point where other congregants feel lost and uninformed about the process.

8. Watch your language! By this I mean your language about the pastor you are seeking. I have read material from search committees that simply "overspiritualize" the process. Did I just say overspiritualize? Yes! The language they use makes it sound as if they are waiting for God to whisper a name in their collective ears, the name of the one who will lead them to the promised land of increased attendance, more pledging, greater church energy, and more spaghetti suppers! All kidding aside, this is a human process and God works through us, fallible human beings who, in turn, call a pastor who is . . . a fallible human being! Please stay grounded. John the Baptist and the Apostle Paul probably won't be in the potential candidate pool—and even they had their flaws!

9. A congregation has to be very deliberate about the why and who of how the Search Committee is put together. This includes calling people with the skills and tasks necessary to facilitate this process.

10. Be very attentive to the efficient use of time and of creating structures that enable you to use time well. Trust your antennae if you feel something is really dragging!

And for the church seeking a part-time pastor: Devote the necessary time to insure full exploration of this topic with prospective candidates, among yourselves, and with the entire church. Beware of communication gaps, and assume nothing!

With all of this as background, let's now consider what a church needs to ask itself in constructing its church profile, what is important for a prospective candidate to ask, and information search committees need to know as a local church considers employing a part-time pastor. These suggestions are spelled out in a different, specific, and detailed format in the appendices. As with all of the material in this book, please consider it and adapt it to the needs of your particular situation.

The Church Profile

One of the most important documents a church can ever construct is the church profile it makes available to those who consider applying to be the church's new pastor. This profile is an opportunity for the church to describe itself, a multifaceted detailing of factual information about financial resources, the physical property and its use, the church's history and heritage, and its goals for both the near and distant future. While some churches such as mine have had considerable experience historically with the realities of a part-time or bivocational minister, for other congregations this is a brand new thing.

The United Church of Christ publishes a profile form that is very helpful to local churches in creating a profile.[3] I have seen this profile used by churches in other traditions as well. While not a perfect document, it is a good model that can be shaped and molded according to the needs of individual churches. Yet, before a profile is published and disseminated, a church with a pastoral vacancy, in this case a vacancy that may be filled with a part-time pastor, will benefit from broad congregational participation in the formation of this profile.

The decision as to who will be involved in establishing this process for the congregation is a crucial one. A denominational official can and should play an integral role. While I am deeply impressed with the profile model established by the UCC and with other models I have read from other denominations, I have not always been as impressed with the way some of the very good profile questions have been answered. Thus I offer several suggestions to local churches in constructing any written document presented to any potential candidate for apart-time pastoral opening:

1. It is vital that the church engage in an in-depth exploration of identity and that responses be stated clearly. While I cannot speak for my entire congregation, I suspect that if they had to construct a profile right now, the term "welcoming congregation" would be their preferred descriptor. Whatever can be done to engage this congregation in identity articulation is crucial!

2. It is important that a church state specifics, not only in terms of its expectations for living out its identity, but also specific, identifiable long- and short-term goals.

3. A church needs to make clear specifically what is expected of its pastor—hours in the office, priorities, and so on.

4. In constructing the profile, the church must avoid generalizations.

5. In constructing the profile, the church needs to cut through euphemistic language and say what it means. I read one profile that called for a pastor whose "preaching style is folksy and who has a good sense of humor." Upon further exploration, I discovered that the translation of that was: "We don't want someone who is going to rock the boat and talk about controversial issues. We want someone who is going to comfort us and make us feel good, just like our old pastor did."

6. It is important in constructing the profile that a church be thorough in constructing questions to which its members will respond. The goal in mind is to elicit the specific concerns and hopes of the congregation with respect to a new pastor. Questions must be constructed well in order to draw these out.

7. If the church is moving from full- to part-time in its pastoral description, it needs to make clear how the congregation feels about that, including an open explanation of discussion and dissent around this issue.

8. With respect to the above, the church has to be clear about any nuances or peculiarities in the church's history that may be related to the present vacancy.

9. If the church is suggesting a part-time pastorate, it also has to spell out for any candidate the specific duties and structuring of work schedules for any other personnel, including administrative assistant, director of Christian education, youth minister, and music director. Expectations for communication among staff members must also be very clear. While applicable to full- and part-time candidates alike, the church's expectations for the pastor as a preacher and worship leader must also steer clear of generalizations. Worship is where most regular congregants encounter the pastor most often.

Any church leader reading this who thinks that the construction of so all encompassing a profile is a daunting task cannot be blamed—it is! How can a congregation ever have the time to think this through and provide the answers an optimal pastoral search would require? The material in the appendices will be helpful, as will the approaches and suggested methodologies I note earlier in this chapter as churches engage in the process, with due respect to their unique needs and the talents of their leaders. Some might see this as slowing down the overall process and running counter to one of the arguments I am making, but if structured well and creatively, this part of the search process could go a long way toward saving overall time. The clarity that will emerge from this valuable reflection should also lead to increased productivity as potential candidates review profiles and as search committees construct and execute their interviews and then move on through their deliberations to make an informed and thorough recommendation for consideration by the church.

SEARCH COMMITTEE INTERVIEWS

By the time a Search Committee has decided to begin interviewing candidates, much significant work should have already been accomplished. With the input of a broad base of those engaged in the life of the church, a thorough profile should have already been developed. Through an organized and streamlined process and constructive discussion regarding the merits of some individual candidates of interest, the committee will have already taken some important steps in determining what might be a good fit for the church. If the preliminary work has been done well, including appropriate reference checks in areas where key questions, including red flags, have arisen, by the time the committee moves to interview mode, it seems reasonable that each candidate being interviewed is seen as the potential new pastor.

This next step in the process therefore is to determine fit. Many factors will play into this. Even with a well-done candidates' profile and a bevy of good references, one cannot adequately judge the way personalities will interact with one another. If a committee leaves an interview with a collective discomfort in this area, that may be a harbinger of less than desirable days ahead. Yet once that hurdle has been cleared the interview serves the purpose of having an in-depth conversation about the church's goals and expectations for itself and its new pastor and about the candidate's strengths and his or her perceptions of this particular church.

Thus the construction of questions for the interview is of high importance. It is here where local denominational officials can be of great help because of their considerable expertise in the area. As preparation for the interviewing process, a mock interview is also desirable as well. This is a chance to test out questions and potential follow-ups. In an era dominated by rubric driven interviews in many fields, including my own field of education, an approach which in essence homogenizes the questions so that each candidate is evaluated against the question itself, the follow-up question continues to be a great source for a deeper understanding of both a candidate's thought process and personality.

Churches considering a part-time and/or bivocational pastor have work to do in addition to the important preparation work that any pastoral search committee needs to do. In crafting their questions, conducting mock interviews, and going through the process with each candidate, the committee must insure that some specific tough questions will be asked that pertain to a part-time approach and its viability in this particular congregation. This interview is most productive if both committee and candidate enter it with a verbalized understanding that, given the nature of the position, they will ask each other the tough questions so that the end result will be most beneficial to all. Even if a particular candidate emerges as a top choice, there will have to be a second interview in which all the nitty-gritty details will be laid out before both committee and candidate.

With all of this in mind, following are some guidelines for a search committee as they prepare to interview candidates to serve as part-time and/or bivocational pastor in their church:

1. All committee members should be prepared to frame inquiries so as to address areas of potential difficulty with this arrangement.

2. When the movement in the church is from full- to part-time staff, it is all the more important that these difficulties be verbalized and questions framed around them.

3. In exploring potential areas of difficulty, committee members must be attentive to concerns expressed by the broadest possible range of members in the congregation.

4. The practical details of hours on-site, office hours, appointments, committee meetings, and the "what if" questions about pastoral emergencies and funerals must be addressed as well as the candidate's assessment of the difficulties inherent in part-time ministry in the church.

5. The committee has to be sure that the potential pastor has laid out in concrete and specific details his or her vision of part-time ministry.

6. It is important to explore a candidate's long-range personal goals and to be sure the committee understands why this candidate is interested in this particular parish at this particular time. Is the potential pastor looking to move this job to full-time? Is this a transitional job in his or her ministerial life, a step along the way to a bigger church? Note: A committee or church may be very comfortable with someone who only wants to be in a church for a short time. Maybe a church needs a jump start and a short-term burst of energy. The baseball afficianado in me would dub this the "hire Billy Martin" approach.[4] It's just important that everyone is clear about intentions!

7. The committee should be prepared to express its understanding about the involvement of the whole church in ministry and question the potential pastor regarding his understanding of what it means to work cooperatively in ministry as part of the priesthood of all believers. The more specifically the implications of the candidate's theology are

spelled out, the more productive the interview and the eventual relationship.

8. The committee needs to ascertain the candidate's willingness to think creatively and his or her energy level regarding the implementation of new ministry initiatives. It is important that churches whose pastoral staff is part-time continue to innovate and address needs without using this part-time status as an excuse to remain stagnant. On more than one occasion, I have seen churches equate downsizing to a part-time pastor with the inevitability that the church will, at best, stagnate and, at worst, die. The antidote to this is a shared passionate commitment to both the current needs and the future of this church—including the congregation's determination to expend the energy necessary to flourish and not decline.

9. It is crucial that the committee come to a specific understanding of how this prospective pastor will seek to be involved in the work of Christian education, youth ministry, and adult education. The small church may not have individuals in staff positions in particular areas of ministry. The candidate may possess strength and expertise in one or more of these areas. It is worth examining how the candidate sees herself or himself getting involved. This raises questions of overall time spent in ministry in the parish and the prioritization of time in terms of both the church's expenditure in paying its pastor and the overall context of a minister's life. For example, will the pastor committed to youth ministry be expected to spend a lot of hours working on retreats, camping trips, youth group meetings, and all of the usual responsibilities of a paid staff member in youth ministry? How does that all fit in to how the minister lives out his or her overall job?

10. It is important to ascertain the candidate's style of conflict management and how he or she sees him- or herself in relation to boards and committees in the church. In small churches where many members take on a variety of roles and people know each other well, much work is done informally. Written processes and procedures and lines of accountability tend not to be as standard as in larger churches. In some churches—my own, for example— pastors have chosen to be engaged in helping the congregation move to more formalized structures and have exerted a take-charge management style as necessary. In a model based on congregational polity this can become an area of great difficulty. It is worth exploring a potential pastor's philosophical approach in this regard and how the candidate sees the parameters of the pastor's role in regard to the smooth management of church affairs, including fiscal matters.

Specific questions addressing these areas of importance are offered in appendix C. It seems that if a search committee is successful in addressing these areas, it will be well on its way toward gaining the information it needs to make a sound recommendation to the entire church. When a community of faith seeks a part-time pastor, it takes on an enormous challenge. The very process in which any church must engage in seeking new leadership is compounded by the part-time configuration. But if search committees structure their time productively, they will be able to gain information needed in order that the church may ultimately grow and benefit as a result of this new configuration for pastoral ministry that they have deliberately chosen.

Suggestions for Part-time or Bivocational Pastoral Candidates

As we have already described, churches considering calling a part-time and/or bivocational minister need to ask some difficult questions both of themselves and of potential candidates. They also have to consider structuring the search process so as to make this viable. Likewise, a candidate seeking such a position must ask the kinds of questions that will provide the information needed to make an informed decision. The stakes for the individual candidate can be rather high.

If this position is a first call, a bad experience can taint this pastor's view of ministry. Depending upon how bad the experience is, an individual's motivation both to serve and to grow in ministry could be severely diminished. A poor job performance, on the other hand, could lead to difficulty in being able to find a satisfying position in the next call or in a subsequent one. This is not to say that a bad experience will ruin one's career in ministry. Many of us have benefited in our lives from the experience we have gained from mistakes. But professional difficulties as well as the inability to serve well can result if the way one is performing on the job is not meeting the spiritual needs of the congregation. Thus common sense and shared human experience dictate the desirability of a satisfactory and successful first call.

The individual seeking to leave a current pastoral position is in a vulnerable position as well. Such a clergyperson might find him- or herself in conversation with a church looking at a part-time pastor as an option. As in other professions, ministers have varied reasons for exploring new job opportunities even as they are currently employed. Some of those reasons follow:

Scaling back: The clergyperson may have been serving in a full-time capacity and is at the point in life in which he or she wishes to move to something else.

Compensation: There is potential for increased salary and/or benefits in the new position. Churches moving from a full-time model to some kind of part-time configuration often scale down compensation packages that are still well beyond what pastors receive in those churches that have called part-time clergy for a while.

Dissatisfaction: The current position is less than satisfying. The usual caveat applies here: Individuals seeking a new position because they are not pleased with their current one must engage in serious self-examination—perhaps with the advisement of a third party such as a counselor, skilled clergy colleague, or spiritual director—to determine any of their own culpability in the circumstances. In colloquial terms, don't carry unnecessary, and harmful, baggage over to a new position.

New challenges: Perhaps this minister is looking for "a new challenge." Many ministers who have been at a church for a while, usually having had a successful ministry there, wonder whether they have done what they have set out to do. Particularly those clergy who see themselves as innovators and agents of change may itch to take on the challenges of a different church. Although change can be good, for the pastor and the congregation, it is important to note that the course of a pastorate goes through different stages, and pastors have found themselves surprised that there may still be exciting work to do after a long term at the same church. The possibilities of innovation and change may even be increased by the trust built over the course of a long-term pastorate. Research on small churches indicates that many ministers leave fairly quickly and move on to greener pastures. The pastor who stays for a longer time might just gain the trust, skills, and knowledge to accomplish amazing and groundbreaking work at that church.

Since about the seventh year of service in my current congregation, I have undergone considerable internal questioning over my term of service. I have been most fortunate to have had a great experience as pastor of my church. Our congregation has done many good things and implemented several significant changes in worship, setting, outreach, and church processes. I have been really pleased with what we have done as a faith community, and the evaluations of the congregation indicate that they have been greatly satisfied as well.

A natural outgrowth of my personality is that I tend to seek new challenges. I've never really been terribly comfortable with the status quo and, over the course of my life, have had issues with religious institutions that I have found to be dull and lifeless. With this baggage of mine in hand, I periodically wonder whether I have done what I can do in a particular place and if it is time to move on and help some other church that seeks to evaluate itself and consider new ways to increase energy, spirit, and a sense of ecclesial community. So, from time to time, I consider the possibility of serving in another church and I have engaged in conversations with denominational officials and search committees about that possibility.

Inevitably, each time I have, not only has there been something about the other congregation that led me to believe it was not the right time for me to go there, but back in my home congregation something happened that made clear that there was still work to be done at home (for home is what my church has become for me). Perhaps someone was going through a difficult time and needed pastoral support. Or perhaps my skills and style were needed to help deal with an organizational or interpersonal matter. Or there was the opportunity for the church to embrace a new program or idea that could benefit the church and those beyond the church walls.

Out of my personal experience, I pose this cautionary question to those who seek a new challenge: Have you underestimated the challenges that remain right where you are? Might you attain greater satisfaction as a pastor by staying put, at least for a little while longer?

I expect that someday I will move on to a different church either in a bivocational capacity or when I retire from my full-time job and perhaps take on a parish as my one and only career. When I do, it will be important that I weigh the challenges available in that new place with the work yet to be done where I am now. I offer this advice to others who might find themselves in a similar situation:

Same hours, better pay: The pastor is looking for a church in which he or she can work approximately the same amount of time, have his or her pastoral skills appreciated, embrace worthwhile challenges . . . and make more money! My only caution is that this pastor owes it to him- or herself and to two congregations, the current and potential new one, to ask all of the right questions—discussed in the preceding text and spelled out in appendices.

The experienced pastor, as well as the first-time pastoral candidate, would benefit not only from reflecting on past experience but also in presenting it as specifically as possible to those involved in making the decision about a possible call to a new congregation. I encourage you to review my "Sample Summary of Bivocational Ministry" in the following section, which I initially wrote for my own self-reflection and as a document to be made available as necessary to another church. In developing this summary, I was forced to spell out in the clearest terms possible what part-time bivocational ministry looks like. Writing it also sent me back to the philosophical underpinnings of the bivocational approach to ministry; much of what you have already read in this book comes from this document.

I suggest that all candidates for a part-time and/or bivocational position write up such a document. The experienced part-time pastor should draw heavily on past experience and make concrete those aspects of the prior call that would be relevant for those looking to have that pastor become their own. I think you will find that my summary provides a prospective new church with specific information upon which to build their questions. In it I covered important topics such as hours on site, pastoral emergencies, and the like, but I also hoped to point to the underlying approach to ministry represented. For greater effectiveness, update your summary from time to time; it is an evolutionary piece of writing, bringing into focus new questions that arise and potential reconsiderations drawn from the real life work of ministry reflected upon well.

Wherever possible, the prospective pastor should consider writing an evaluation of his or her approach to ministry in relationship to what he or she has read in the seeking church's profile. Pastoral candidates read profiles carefully and formulate questions from those readings. I encourage them to take this a bit further and comment upon what they have read about a church's needs and directly draw comparisons between that and their own vision of and approach to ministry within that particular church. This brings both the prospective employer and potential pastor away from the realm of ethereal, speculative discussion and into the specifics of what this individual pastor might bring to this particular parish in the most concrete way possible.

SAMPLE SUMMARY OF BIVOCATIONAL MINISTRY

As you have seen, ours is a very active church and I am very involved in leading and facilitating programs within it. Since I was called to my church in 2001, my congregation has been comfortable in adapting to the fact that I am bivocational, as I have described in detail throughout my profile. I know that members of my congregation will attest that I am not only accessible but also actively involved in the workings of the church on a day-to-day basis, even though I am not physically present through traditional office hours. In a typical week, I work between twenty-five and thirty hours in my capacity as pastor. In certain weeks, that goes up to close to forty. My congregation has not asked me to do time sheets or time cards and is deeply trusting that I am carrying out my responsibilities thoroughly. Here is how we have structured this:

As much as possible, we make maximum use of Sunday mornings for meetings and educational programming. I on occasion come out for other meetings as necessary. These are all planned very carefully.

I am available for individual meetings by appointment based on mutual convenience and am responsive to requests for home and hospital visits. I think you would find that members of my congregation are most pleased with my pastoral responsiveness.

I communicate regularly and with great frequency with my congregation through e-mail updates. I'd be pleased to provide upon request an example of a typical update. I also am in regular contact with our congregation leaders regarding committee work and worship planning. Our website is highly utilized and a strong vehicle for communication. I have developed a blog, which provides opportunity for deeper exploration of issues discussed and preached about at worship. I am currently exploring the possibilities of increased use of updated technological forms (such as Twitter). We have established communication channels for those in the congregation not engaged in Internet use. I am very available for phone calls at home, and people affiliated with our congregation are given my cell phone number as well. This contact information is published in our newsletter, which is mailed to all residents of our town and those in other locations who have made connections and formed a relationship with our church.

I type the worship bulletin at home and it is e-mailed to one of our deacons by Wednesday of each week. We have no secretarial help.

Of course, I spend extensive time at home in sermon preparation and in ongoing worship planning with our music director and the large number of people who share worship leadership.

What you do not see in all of this is the traditional daytime office hours arrangement, but I think that I am highly accessible to my parishioners.

Ministry in Union, Connecticut, February 2001–Present

I would describe this period as one marked by a great increase in spiritual energy and vitality. This was noted in the church's own self-evaluation, which I requested, and in the regular evaluations related to my doctoral work. Some indicators of this include:

- Increase in the number of people assuming leadership roles within the community and thus expanding the "core group" of leaders.

- Increase in the number of people volunteering to do active work in the church and to actually lead activities.

- Notable increase in activities our church offers the community: We have brought in musicians for concerts and established a traditional fall dinner and Christmas Fair as a result of this vitality.

- Strong increase in our multigenerationality and a growth in multigenerational programming.

- Establishment of Family Worship Sundays in order to "grow the middle" of the church and to try to solidify the church's relevance to the broadest possible local population.

- Stronger and intentional connections to the United Church of Christ through active participation on the association, regional, and conference levels. This also includes strong involvement in 2007 General Synod.

- With appropriate recognition to the size of the town (at slightly more than seven hundred, the smallest town in Connecticut), significant growth in church attendance and in giving.

It is important to note that when I came to this church in 2001, I was the beneficiary of the outstanding work of pastors before me and the amazing commitment of that congregation to the work of the local church. While I understand that, due to the confidential nature of this process, you can't directly access information from my church, I am confident that my regional minister will attest to the fact that my relationship with the congregation has been and is excellent and has been marked by mutual respect. They have been and are deeply supportive of me and I, in turn, am most grateful.

Specific developments since 2001

- Completion of handicapped access project with two fully functional chair lifts, one to our sanctuary and one to our parish hall.

- Purchase of new hymnal, keyboard, and new large print New Revised Standard Version Bibles as well as a new NRSV pulpit Bible.

- Recent approval of purchase of a new organ with money donated to church.

- Changes within the sanctuary to include baptismal font, appropriate banners and liturgical table coverings, and changes in paraments for worship. In addition, we have done some reconfiguration of our worship space.

- Development of blended worship, utilizing both traditional and contemporary music.

- Revitalization of our choir and considerable increase in frequency of their offerings and in their numbers. Development and growth of a children's choir and an increase in soloists and groups providing different kinds of worship music, including some original compositions.

- Establishment of a music director position.

- Guest speakers at worship, including our conference minister and regional minister.

- Guest musicians and a proliferation of creative work, both written and musically, among members of our congregation

- Implementation of new worship approaches, often drawn from United Church of Christ *Book of Worship.*

- Through my doctoral program, involvement of congregation in sermon development and evaluation. This has continued after completion of my degree as well.

- Welcoming Initiative: our church delivers welcome baskets to all new residents of Union, including information about our church.

- Growth in adult education, including moving some programs to a local breakfast spot and varied methods/options both within and outside of worship. Employment of discussion time on occasion as part of services. Introduction of congregational "Summer Reading" programs, which have included the titles *Religious Literacy, Life Together, Lest Innocent Blood Be Shed, Amish Grace,* and *The Future of Faith.*

- Establishment of film series and discussions, expansion of available reading materials in church, and development of a reading/sharing table.

- Occasional use of appropriate video clips in worship.

- Many sermon series on significant topics, including recent "Back to the Bible" series. Integration of sermon series with educational initiatives.

- Regular articles written by the pastor and used as bulletin inserts on theological topics and issues within the church.

- Growth of music opportunities for all ages.

- Establishment of active youth ministry program, including creative youth worship, retreats, and mission projects

- Development of youth leadership, including two high school students serving on the Board of Deacons.

- Ongoing involvement of youth in worship leadership.

- Integrating long-range planning into the budget process, which included a churchwide retreat and the establishment per bylaws of a Fiscal Oversight Committee to facilitate on-going planning and conversation. These were initiatives presented by the pastor, who also convened what had been a dormant church committee at a time of fiscal crisis and helped facilitate the development of new published policies and procedures for the church.

- Recent acceptance of a comprehensive policy on gifts. (Note: This was an outgrowth of a controversy surrounding a gift. I would be happy to explain further, as I believe it offers insight into how I deal with conflict.)

- Change in wedding policies to allow blessings of civil unions in 2005 and same-sex marriages in 2009, after the change in Connecticut law went into effect.

- Establishment of the "All Are Welcome" theme and integration of that theme into what we give our guests: laminated cards, bookmarks, pens, magnets (examples available upon request) and reinforced in the church newsletter and website, and on my blog.

- Expansion of our newsletter, which goes to all town residents, and an electronic option for our newsletter (accessible on the website).

- Establishment and expansion of our website, www.unioncc.com. We have received much positive feedback about this site and people have visited our church as a result of it.

- Implementation of a blog, which is integrated with our education and worship: http://wwwpastorbob.blogspot.com.

- Church involvement (eight members) in an important new regional small church consultation initiative. I have served as committee member, preacher, and presenter at various consultations.

- Development of "Service of Remembrance for Those Who Have Died," offered annually during Advent, and use of "Rite of Healing" (*UCC Book of Worship*), offered each Advent and Lent.

- Significant attendance growth at holiday worship and development of increased worship leadership involvement.

- Establishment of Laity Sunday as an important annual worship experience; development of creative approaches to preaching during this service.

- Hosting of our association Annual Meeting and Executive Council.

- Recognition in 2006, 2007, and 2008 as a UCC "Five for Five" church.

- Involved on a multigenerational level in the work of Simply Smiles, an orphanage for children in Mexico (www.simplysmiles.org).

- In response to a fiscal crisis necessitating budgetary cuts, implementation of a plan to insure continued giving to various worthwhile causes.

While this is not a complete listing of the work we have done, I offer it as a starting point for ongoing conversation as we continue the journey that is this search process.

Summary

As a church seeks a part-time and/or bivocational minister, it is critical that all parties involved take the opportunity to formulate real-life questions regarding what such a ministry might look like in the local congregation and what realistic expectations for a pastor in such a situation might be. It is my hope that this chapter and the appendices elaborating on the contents therein will serve useful to all as they pursue this important decision.

〜

Discussion Questions:

1. Comment specifically on the pros and cons of any of the author's concrete suggestions.

2. Evaluate the worth of providing a detailed summary of one's vision of part-time or bivocational ministry. How might it be helpful or counterproductive in the search and call process?

3. The author is quite critical of the way many search committees function. Please comment on this in light of your own experiences.

7

Successful Part-time and Bivocational Ministry

As is the case with so many frequently used words in our language, one must move rather quickly to definition, description, or explanation. Each Advent, for example, I struggle with the words we use when we engage in the simple act of lighting candles: hope, peace, joy, love. These words beg for clarification lest their power and impact be lost because they are used so casually and can so easily become so trite. So it is with the word "success" as it is applied to ministry. Any church seeking a new minister wants that minister to be a success (the "clergy killer" phenomenon aside![1]), and any minister who seeks out a church most certainly wants to be successful as well.

Part of the ongoing discernment and discussion within churches, as well as between and within candidates and those churches, needs to center on what constitutes success. Likewise, those groups who seek to assist churches and candidates in this process, such as denominational officials and seminary professors and advisors, need to grapple with this issue as well. The following indicators of successful part-time, bivocational ministry do not constitute an all-encompassing list but should provide a framework through which you might draw upon your resources to most completely and thoroughly explore the meaning of success in the context in which we have been discussing it:

- The congregation as a whole feels that their pastoral needs are being met.
- The congregation experiences the pastor's interest in the church.
- The congregation is aware of a positive energy marking the life of the church and a sense of meaning found through the church's worship and preaching.
- The pastor feels that he or she is affirmed by the congregation and that her or his pastoral skills are being well utilized.

Some might say this short listing is too general and leaves several necessary areas untouched. Might it not be possible that a successful pastorate would include at least some of the following?

- Increased attendance.
- Increased financial giving.
- Increased membership.
- Increased youth involvement.
- Improvements in the church's physical plant.
- Increased volunteerism within the church, with more people taking on responsibilities for the church's life.
- Development of new programs, even necessitating consideration of expanding staff.

- Recognition by the denomination as a congregation moving in the right direction.

- Enough growth that might one day necessitate a full-time pastor.

A word of caution to churches and ministers alike: It is really important to be very careful when defining success in terms of numbers or money. Recognize also not only that most part-time ministries we have been describing will of necessity take place in "small" churches, but also that there is enormous strength attached to being a small church.

For example, by reading my vision of bivocational ministry in the previous chapter, you probably got a taste of what life is like in our small congregation, a faith community I will go on a limb and call a "success." Were you to stop by our church on a typical Sunday morning, you would not fight off the hundreds of cars you might at a typical megachurch. Were you to walk into our church, you'd find yourself worshiping with a group of about forty or so other individuals.

I think that as you pulled up to our building you would be impressed by the number of young people you would see on the property, and I think you'd get a sense that there is a good mix of ages. If you were to peruse our bulletin, I think you'd be impressed by the wide range of activities—concerts, dinners, educational opportunities, and so on available for all ages. If you came to worship with us, I think you'd like the way our sanctuary looks and the variety of music we sing and the energy and passion with which we sing it. I also sense that on certain Sundays you'd be amazed at the size and quality of our choir and the willingness of individuals to express their talents so well and creatively. I can also only hope that you would find the preached Word to have a positive impact on your life; evaluations we have done indicate that it has done so for many.

My sense, though, is that if you were looking with a bottom-line mindset, you might wonder: Where is the money? Why no more bodies in the seats? But I believe that the small church carries with it a unique power within the broader ecclesiastical world. I will even go so far as to say that there is something ideal about the small setting, something that good large churches have replicated well—for example, the infusion of base groups and Small Christian Communities movements in larger churches as well as small groups formed around certain issues, worship styles, and study topics.

Churches ought to be comfortable with their smallness and move beyond any inferiority complex about it. Some factors are beyond the control of churches in this regard: the changing place of religion in American life, demographic and population shifts, the advent and development of new religious movements, and many more. The simple reality is that most Americans are not in any church of any size on Sunday morning. Thus rather than bemoaning what it is not, the small church needs to cherish and affirm what it is in the current religious configuration of this nation—a magnificent gift!

PASTORAL CHALLENGES UNIQUE TO THE SMALL CHURCH

The part-time and/or bivocational minister needs to recognize that serving a small church involves several unique challenges. First and foremost is usually the ongoing financial challenge, which can limit the staffing options that a church has. As you may have noticed in my description of my church, we have no secretary, our music director has been part-time with limited hours and a modest stipend, and paying a youth minister has been discussed but not implemented due to financial issues.

A pastor must therefore decide how her or his skills can best meet current pastoral needs. Because of my background in youth ministry, I have assumed some responsibility for the formation of our youth programs over the years. In churches where the minister's strengths or interests are not in that area, the church would need another solution. Even in a situation such as mine, an individual church and pastor have to assess the benefits of having the bivocational, part-time pastor, who holds down a full-time job, spend Friday nights sleeping on a bean bag chair on his church office floor when he has other pastoral duties to perform, such as preaching at the congregation's Sunday service.

In my experience, however, one of the great challenges facing the small church is the fact that there really is so much to do just to keep a church running and even more so to keep it running well, and there are so few people willing to assume leadership positions on boards and committees of the church. We all know what this reality can lead to an increased workload on the part of those involved, heightened frustration and fatigue by those who do a lot for the church, often manifesting as bitterness and a tendency to lash out at those in the church who don't seem to be pulling their weight or doing their share.

Set up as a backdrop to all of this is a part-time pastor who may have a full-time job or some other job that keeps her or him busy with oodles of other responsibilities. This has the potential to become a real mess: Busy members of the congregation might feel that the pastor is not doing enough and is shirking responsibilities by passing them on to others. The pastor might feel that others, often the busiest people in the congregation, are not doing enough and are failing to show him or her support.

This could really get ugly if not dealt with well! To do effective small church ministry, a pastor needs an educational background that includes development of strong conflict resolution skills, because conflict will take place in small congregations if positive programs are to take place. Now, because many Christian folk see conflict as unbecoming the image of "being a good Christian," what often happens is that necessary organizing and structuring gets put on the back burner because people don't want to stir up the pot. In essence, everyone politely recognizes that everyone is busy, so therefore it is okay if things do not get done.

The flip side of this situation is that the church is not attracting new people, or the congregation is aging and people are not being replaced. Congregants may be simmering inside that congregational leaders aren't doing enough to stem the tide. But those same congregants, without consciously knowing it, have developed a deep-down complacency—an understanding that "this is the way it is in our little church." Lay leaders, meanwhile, grow frustrated that "people don't want change" and "nothing is ever going to get done."

My conviction, based on both training and experience, is that a small church pastor must have two specific skill sets, conflict resolution and executive management or delegation of responsibilities.

A pastor can move a congregation beyond the paralysis of inaction if he or she is comfortable with helping them manage the inevitable conflicts that might result from the very process of effecting change.

A pastor in a small church has to be very comfortable with what I would describe as executive management skills—taking charge and moving and inspiring people to assume and fulfill leadership positions and other duties well.

The latter conviction might meet with resistance because on the surface it seems to contradict a solid Protestant conviction that the church belongs in the hands of the laypeople, not the pastor. This certainly is the case with my congregation, which dates back to pre-Revolutionary days before there was a state of Connecticut, much less a United States of America. Other Protestants in different places and denominations might have a higher comfort level with the strong pastor image but still maintain that the notion of a priesthood of all believers fully implies ownership and direction of the church by the people, not the pastor. When push comes to shove, after all, even beyond New England Congregationalism, Protestantism has mechanisms in place for a pastor's removal.

Yet I strongly believe that there are times in a small church when a pastor has to get people to move. There is not one style of doing this. I have a background as an athletic coach, having led varsity high school teams that have won conference championships and done well in state competition. When the situation warrants, I can flex my coach-like, "take-charge" muscles. I can be quite verbal and argumentative when necessary. In doing so, I try to keep my civility and respect for others intact! Other leaders, strong leaders indeed, might be far quieter than I am and still move people to action.

There are many ways of practicing executive management skill, and there are times when a small church pastor just has to do it. In my current position there have been two occasions when I was deeply concerned that unless we put some structures in place, we could experience crippling financial difficulties that might sap the spiritual vitality of our church, rendering it unattractive to those who might consider seeking us out.

In the first instance, I outlined to members of our boards and committees a proposed new structure for our church in which we would establish a Fiscal Oversight Committee to do detailed budget planning and to focus that planning on the spiritual priorities of the church. As a pastor, I cannot require a new structure, but can only offer spiritual opportunities. So, concurrent with my proposal, I extended an invitation to the entire church to participate in an evening churchwide retreat in which we would not discuss money. But instead of calling it a budget retreat, I labeled it our "hopes, dreams, and visions" event, words drawn deliberately from the self-identification hymn "All Are Welcome." (The sequence of events leading up to this event and the relationship between the two initiatives might be clearer when you read my sermon "The Most Dreaded Sermon," found in appendix D.)

On another, more recent occasion, it seemed obvious to me as well as to others reporting to me that if we were going to make the best use of our financial resources and maximize the results from our varied budgetary and fund-raising initiatives—do our best to save energy costs and plan well and effectively for the future—we had to move to a more modernized system of processing our offerings and providing information to our congregation. Unless we got a tighter grip on these processes, the potential for frustration might grow and have damaging results. In reviewing our bylaws, I was drawn to the existence of an entity called simply the "Church Committee," which brought people together from the different boards and committees to make decisions about the church.

In my years as pastor, this committee had not been utilized, as those who comprise it were on the other appropriate committees that needed to get the church's work done. I asked our lay leader if he would be willing to convene a meeting of the Church Committee, which he did. At our initial meeting, I proposed some structural, procedural changes, church leaders commented on these proposals, and I agreed to take the responsibility for piecing our common work together in a draft document that would then be shaped and molded at our next meeting.

The end result was positive action, and what was agreed upon was the shared result of our common work. It was not a matter of rubber-stamping the pastor's initiative. As a result of our deliberations, the committee felt that this group really needed to be revitalized and to meet on a regular basis to monitor the overall work of the church. I think that this has contributed to a feeling that the enormous burdens of leadership in a small church is being shared by those gathered around the table, a table open to new leaders joining us as well.

My executive management actions in this case consisted of:

1. Analyzing the situation and suggesting that we meet.
2. Offering proposals during our meeting.
3. Contributing to our common discussion and extending a willingness to facilitate it.
4. Offering to utilize my writing ability and theological background to craft a document.
5. Contributing to the final shaping of a document that was agreed upon by consensus.

At every step along the way it was important to me that decisions were reached jointly. The process requires some background in management and administration, and here my experience in public schools—responsibility for chairing meetings, dealing with parent-teacher conferences, and implementing individualized plans for students—was readily transferable to the church setting. My bivocational situation was really able to benefit the congregation. Likewise, other bivocational pastors would likely bring significant gifts from their other training and experience that could be just what their congregations need at a particular time.

The small church quite often runs informally and, as is the case with most strengths, that can also be a downside as well. Early in my pastorate, I noticed that certain agreed-upon projects were not moving along particularly quickly. My impatience with the "wouldn't it be nice if?" mindset led me to wonder how to spur movement on so many necessary initiatives, often involving minute details. I found that I could contribute to quicker resolutions by raising questions at committee meetings and by working directly with the individuals taking responsibility for a particular project. The list of changes described in my "Sample Summary of Bivocational Ministry" in chapter 6 were the result of hard work done, not by me, but rather by members of the congregation.

However, I was very much involved in helping to prioritize where that work fit into the life of the congregation.

If a pastor exhibits executive management skill, he or she can help liberate the person volunteering by enabling that person to give his or her responsibilities the proper focus for the right amount of time. By convening groups of congregants to discuss their common needs, the pastor can contribute to individuals' sense that they need not feel overwhelmed but can play their part in the shared responsibilities of those who choose to serve their local church.

Those of us who work in institutional structures are quite familiar with how bureaucracy can slow down not only progress and change but also, in many cases, basic, necessary functioning. Big institutions can suffer from the inertia that can result from multilayered bureaucracy, so complex that one sometimes does not really know who really made what decision. But smaller institutions, including churches, can be slowed down by the fact that a limited number of people are stretched so thin that decisions and actions that need to be made in a timely manner are all too often unnecessarily deferred. A pastor with solid management skills can help a parish cut through a lot of red tape!

In the small church, the pastor should also be trained in and comfortable with the art and science of conflict resolution. To be as straightforward as one can be, a small church does not have that many members, much less people who are directly involved in an active, hands-on way. If a major blowup develops between just two individuals, that disagreement may contain within itself the potential to rupture the entire body, in this case, the body of Christ, as scripture describes the church.

It is pretty obvious why these disagreements and tensions may arise—deeply caring people, with umpteen nonchurch responsibilities, may feel overworked and underappreciated. When they do, the last thing the congregation needs is a pastor who will either pretend the conflict doesn't exist, wish it away, or, maybe even worse, try to "pray it away," resorting to some disembodied spirituality that, quite frankly, only serves to mask the fact that people are really angry and often quite hurt! Two people in a small church who are mad at each other may lead to others choosing up sides, increasing discomfort among parishioners and quite likely causing once involved individuals to leave the church or to refuse to invest in it emotionally. People experiencing or witnessing the conflict may become embittered, souring them on the church as a place where Christian values are put into practice.

When conflict among congregants happens,, it is natural for the pastor to be angry and resentful. He or she might come to think that words spoken from the pulpit, words like peace and forgiveness and reconciliation, are all nothing more than hollow, empty pious religious platitudes—that what the pastor preaches has absolutely no effect on how people behave, and that the church is really like all other human institutions, no better and, because of its great ideals, quite often worse!

Here the pastor must get a grip! The pastor must be willing to take control, recognizing that he or she might have the skills and philosophical inclination to help people work through this conflict rather than run away from it. The Christian minister, grounded in the heart of biblical theology, should be the first to understand and recognize that we all, minister included, are flawed human beings. In fact, we are sinners and, in keeping with the biblical understanding of sin, we know that our behavior and our attitudes so often miss the mark. The pastor then has the unique opportunity to exercise what scripture alludes to as "the ministry of reconciliation," not by putting one's head in the sand but by helping people in their process of healing, knowing that the rupture in the body is being transformed and healed as well. As Henri Nouwen told us so beautifully, the skilled minister knows that we all carry wounds.[2] Jesus did and we do. It follows logically that so does the church of Jesus Christ in all of its local expressions. We are wounded. The minister is wounded, yet is called to be a wounded healer, for the sake of the body of Christ. And the first step in treating the wound, my friends, is to recognize that there is a wound!

Training for Bivocational and Part-Time Ministry

Knowledge of the skills needed to serve as a part-time and/or bivocational pastor does not happen overnight. Seminaries charged with helping to prepare candidates to serve as ordained clergy need to be attentive to this emerging need in structuring appropriate pastoral programs. The seminaries affiliated with mainline denominations have done an excellent job historically in responding to the needs of a changing church and have responded to those needs with outstanding opportunities for both pastoral practice and the opportunity for shared reflection. As they seek to serve the needs of the future church, a church in which the ministries we have described in this book may very well continue to burgeon in the congregational life of our nation, they must continue to regularly reexamine how what they are offering in their curricula will best serve church needs as they shall continue to evolve.

To this end, I offer the following suggestions to seminaries working with denominations and to denominational officials who are asked to consult with seminaries regarding suggestions for quality training of their seminarians.

- ❧ If a seminarian expresses interest in pursuing the possibility of either part-time or bivocational ministry, it is important that his or her training program include opportunities to interact with those who serve in those capacities. This interest should be taken into consideration when internship and practicum programs are set up for prospective clergy.

- ❧ It would be advisable for denominational polity courses to include readings on current and projected congregational trends in the area of part-time ministry, as well as information on trends in the wider church.

- Guest speakers for classes and for the larger seminary community should include those who could be helpful in exposing seminarians to the complexities of bivocational ministry within the current and future church.

- Local denominational offices (diocesan, conference, and the like) should work to insure that opportunities are provided for their clergy and local churches to learn more about various available options in part-time ministry. Workshops might be offered at denominational meetings and materials made available to people on the local level.

- Those who serve in consultative capacities within denominations should pay careful attention to trends in part-time ministry and find ways to incorporate this information into conversations with local churches and search committees as needs arise within those congregations.

- Local settings within denominations should consider offering programs that address the needs of small churches. These programs, in many cases, may even be more effective if they are conducted ecumenically.

One of the finest experiences I have had as a small church pastor has been being part of a series of small church programs in our denomination's Eastern Region of our state. As a result of the vision of our conference's regional minister, we formed a committee, of which I was a member, that sought to bring representatives from many local small churches together for structured programs and discussions on a wide variety of topics that concerned small churches. Among the many topics discussed were the financial realities of life in the small churches trenches, with problematic, often deficit budgets, declining attendance, and real pastoral need. These small church gatherings, held either within one's denomination or ecumenically, would serve as outstanding settings for serious discussions about the issues surrounding part-time ministry. They might even serve as catalysts for some creative solutions to perceived problems on the local level.

The bottom line in all of this is that issues related to part-time ministry within local churches need to be addressed systematically and officially. In my view, there is currently a dearth of materials available on this topic, especially concerning churches within the mainline denominations. It is incumbent among seminaries and denominational offices to provide consultative and educational services to both seminarians and local churches regarding issues and trends in this area. As has always been the case, each individual seminarian needs to discern where her or his strengths may best be utilized once this seminarian becomes part of the ordained clergy of a particular denomination. An honest evaluation of the issues involved in part-time ministry requires that seminaries and denominations do their jobs well in this regard.

A recurring educational issue, discussed earlier, centers on educational training for those entering part-time ministry. This is especially relevant if an individual is considering ministry while employed in another career. Those charged with overseeing training and certification for ordination must hold in balance the importance of strong theological and pastoral training with the real life needs of those who could serve the church well. The training program for the permanent diaconate in the Roman Catholic Church in which I participated many years ago is an interesting model that could be shaped and adapted by Protestant seminaries and denominations.

When I was accepted as a prospective candidate for ordination as a deacon, I held a full-time position as a teacher in a school. In addition, I was also a baseball coach at that school. I was accepted into a class with nine other candidates, most of whom held full-time jobs as well. The Archdiocese of Hartford had arranged for a training program consisting of the equivalent of thirty credit hours over a four-year period, with classes held each Wednesday evening at a centralized spot in the Archdiocese, with classes taught by clergy and laity well trained in the particular disciplines encompassed within our curriculum.

In addition, my particular class of candidates was required to engage in a supervised pastoral ministry (for example, hospital visitation, parish religious education, youth ministry, work with the homeless, and the like) over the course of the academic year. In my own training, I worked in three different areas of pastoral ministry. Within the year, we also attended three weekend workshops on specific topics related to issues confronting the church and did a full weekend candidates' retreat. We were also required to engage in spiritual direction, and our participation in this had to be verified.

Our course work encompassed scripture, ethics, worship, spirituality, church history, prayer, the specifics of liturgical leadership, homiletics, and several other areas relevant to our future ministry as ordained clergy. Most of us completed this curriculum while retaining our full-time jobs and family responsibilities.

Is it possible for candidacy committees and those charged with overseeing the education of clergy to look at this kind of model to see if it might need the needs of the modern church for part-time ministers? Again, this is a model that can be shaped and augmented as necessary, but is it not possible that seminaries and denominations working together on this could create structures that not only meet the needs of potential part-time ministers, but are also beneficial to the local church?

There should be no shortcuts in this educational approach. It is important that the following elements be both present and operative:

- Solid academic training in theology, biblical studies, and related disciplines.
- Quality spiritual direction and discernment opportunities.

- Immersion in the life of the denomination and reflected-upon experience in the local settings of that denomination.

- The formation of in depth collegial opportunities as candidates grow together as future ministers.

It is my sense that this can be effected creatively without requiring ministers in training to leave their jobs and enroll full-time in an Master of Divinity program in a seminary. Those who would express concern that students on this alternative track would be segregated from other seminarians raise a valid point. Opportunities should therefore be provided through the denominations and seminaries working with them to bring candidates together for dialogue and shared learning. In doing so, denominational leaders and seminary staff contribute greatly to the education of the church's future leaders, as full-time and part-time clergy shall be called upon to interact well with one another for the well-being of the church.

THE ELEPHANT IN THE ROOM: RESISTANCE FROM CLERGY

A few years ago, I was having a conversation with a few other small church pastors in which I made the comment that, given the realities, financial and otherwise, of the emerging church, many churches that currently have full-time pastors might benefit from considering a part-time leadership model. My comment was not met with enthusiasm from a full-time pastor of a church not much bigger than my own. This is not an uncommon position. I have encountered many pastors out there who honestly believe that in the majority of churches, including the one they happen to be serving right now, pastoral ministry is best exercised as a full-time job. They see some of the current trending toward alternative considerations as a diminution of ministerial service within the local congregation, and they are resistant.

While job security is certainly a piece in this puzzle, there is much more to this than self-centered motivation. There is honest conviction that, where possible, churches are best served by full-time clergy. And, as stated earlier in this book, I agree with them. Where we might differ, though, is in our willingness to evaluate the "where possible" dimension, for I also happen to believe that there exist churches, perhaps a good number, that, because of a variety of circumstances, need to reevaluate whether they really need a full-time pastor. It is in the best interest of the contemporary and future church for its clergy to be open to the reality that local churches need to evaluate what configurations of leadership best work for them, and that evaluation could lead to the conclusion that it's time to look at a part-time, maybe even bivocational, pastor.

In offering this opinion, I wish to contribute to the "where possible" discussion by stating the following:

1. Wherever possible, the local congregation benefits from having full-time clergy on staff.

2. Local churches are not exempt from the obligations of justice, and that includes how the church treats its clergy. It is important to be very specific here: If a minister has received a call to serve a church as a full-time pastor, that church has made a contractual and, I would argue, covenantal agreement to receive full-time pastoral services. This covenant is a very serious one between a pastor and a church.

3. (This is where things get sticky.) What if a church is discovering that it is getting harder and harder to pay the full-time salary? What if finances are declining? I would argue that so long as the pastor wishes to remain and he or she is evaluated well by the congregation, the church has the obligation to work arduously so that the terms of the agree-

ment may be upheld. Here is where ethical obligations on the part of the congregation really come into play. In no way, shape, or form should anybody seek to force that pastor out by stirring up negative evaluative material, piling on extra responsibilities that make it hard for the pastor to fulfill responsibilities within the parish, or engaging in any other kind of pernicious move to encourage the pastor to leave. That would simply be unethical. This is not to say that people whom the pastor trusts in the congregation should not have serious and honest conversations with the pastor about the dilemmas caused by this situation. The end result of these conversations might even be that the pastor voluntarily suggests that he or she move to a different status or comes to a realization that in the best interest of one's self, family, and church, it is best to seek out a new call, retire a bit early, or whatever might make sense depending upon the pastor's age and stage in life. This is all very delicate and must be treated as such!

4. In fairness to, and in support of, the important relationship between pastor and congregation, a congregation should never switch a job description until an opening occurs in the parish unless the overwhelming confluence of circumstances make this a last and necessary resort. When a pastoral opening occurs is the natural time for the church to engage in a reevaluation of itself anyway. How the position of pastor is to be funded is tied in, as we have described, to the multiplicity of other issues facing the congregation. As a church is evaluating itself and the place of the pastor within it, the church needs to spell out exactly what the role of the pastor is in terms of the overall ministry of the church. An interim pastor can be very helpful in consulting with a church through this process.

Those reading this book are well aware, I am sure, that people in every professional position hold to images of what that position is that have been shaped by training and practice over a period of time. Professional clergy are not exempt from this. Many are very clear about what it means to function as a pastor in a full-time role: Hold office hours, be available for pastoral counseling, meet with other clergy, attend denominational meetings, do hospital and convalescent home calls, be available to respond on a moment's notice to an emergency, be available for prayer breakfasts and daytime Bible study, be present in the civic community of which the congregation is a part. These are all good things and hard to argue against. Yet just as other professions have changed and as professional business people have discovered that, by using the Internet, teleconferencing, and basic business conference calling, productivity can be at least as good as if one were to spend thousands more shipping personnel all over the country or globe, so too perhaps ministry in a church can be done as well by being open to the use of other methods and models.

The traditional full-time minister will likely object to my contention on both a visceral and intellectual level, arguing perhaps that I am on a slippery slope of depersonalization within the congregation. The minister and congregation could run the risk of interacting in simple transactional ways without the kind of personal touch that makes the work of the clergy what it is. I wholeheartedly endorse that concern.

My counter argument is that the current setup does not necessarily meet the desired end of relational personalism either. While the minister is sitting in his or her office from 9:00 A.M. to 4:00 P.M., with breaks for lunch and special meetings and often with other ministers, where is most of the congregation? They are at work and not in the position to meet with the minister. They might seek the pastor at a time that does not interfere with the workday or with family responsibilities.

It is possible in professional ministry to run into the problem one runs into in professional anything, that is, things have to be this way because they have always been. I see this all the time in my other line of work. Technological advances have shaped the ways in which teachers interact with students as well as the expectations for how professional staff may need to interact with parents. This is not a book about professional education so I will spare you the citations of numerous examples from the world of public schools. Suffice it to say that the professions I entered in 1974 as a teacher and 1989 as a counselor have different job descriptions now than they did then, as does the professional work of interscholastic coaching. One should not be surprised that this might apply to the work of professional ministry too.

One of the best educational periods in my life included the three summer residencies I spent in Chicago as part of an ecumenical Doctor of Ministry in Preaching program through the Association of Chicago Theological Schools. Apart from the wonderful classroom educational experience these residency periods provided, I learned a lot from living among those who did ministry work full-time. Through my many discussions with them, I learned a lot about the lived Protestant clergy experience. I had known a lot of full-time Roman Catholic priests, but because of church policy on mandatory celibacy, the reality of Catholic rectory living was different from that of my colleagues, many of whom had spouses, partners, or children. As a bivocational minister, I found the exchange and dialogue between and among us to be really helpful in my ministry, and I hope my friends have found it to be in theirs as well.

I also discovered that in the ministry, as in other professions, there is a culture within which one operates, a culture that has set many expectations, educationally and professionally. There is a pattern to being a minister into which people are absorbed. In professional ministry, this usually means residential seminary education at one of the denomination's seminaries or one approved by it and a fairly set way of structuring one's time within the pastoral setting, an organizational structure learned through seminary field education placements and internships. Having supervised interns as a school counselor, I understand firsthand what this process entails. A major part of any worthwhile internship is the process of learning and adapting to the culture of that job. In itself, there is nothing wrong with that, nothing at all.

In fact, if someone who has been inculcated within this system and has been successful within it—someone who believes that this model really serves the needs of parishioners and other community members—sees that there is a movement away from this model, it is not unusual that the person both question it and be concerned that a different way of doing things could lead to lessened pastoral service. While there will always be those in the ministry, as with any other profession, who know that they could do just as much part-time as they do now, the reality is that most full-time pastors work very hard and find themselves not having enough hours in a day or week to do all that they really need to do. Any argument that churches might consider looking at part-time ministry is not meant to negate the importance of full-time ministry within the local church or to deny that it is the ideal. It is to suggest instead that new realities call for new solutions, and leaders in the church do the church no justice by seeing themselves as exempt, by staying stuck in an old model.

CONCLUSION

In the ideal world, a local church would benefit from a well balanced staff which could meet the spiritual needs of the congregation and wider community. A full-time pastor is a great benefit to the local church and its ministry of presence within the wider community. Most congregations would benefit from other individuals who would spend a great deal of time on church matters and be well and justly compensated for their professional work. This would include an administrative assistant, director of Christian education, youth minister, pastoral counselor, pastoral care coordinator, and coordinator of maintenance, as well as those holding responsibilities associated with those positions, whether under these or other titles. The reality is that congregations generally have limited resources and, because of the limitations within which they have to live, are forced to make decisions about how best to formulate a staff so as to meet the real needs of the local church.

I have tried to make the case throughout this book that many congregations, including some which have traditionally and historically supported full-time pastors, have moved or will move into the position wherein they must look at the possibility of calling a part-time pastor instead, perhaps even one who must hold down another job in order to pay his or her bills and provide for oneself and those to whom one is responsible. I have tried to make it clear that whether a pastor is part- or full-time, the local church itself has full-time pastoral needs and it is the obligation of the entire congregation to decide how those full-time needs will be met.

I have tried to identify the resistance some might have to moving away from traditional organizational structures while implying that for many churches a shift in structure is both inevitable and desirable. I have sought to offer suggestions to denominational officials, local churches, and the committees that consider pastoral candidates as to how best to examine a church's pastoral needs and to articulate the role of the pastor in responding to the needs in a particular concretely rooted congregation.

In offering suggestions to church officials, local churches, and seminaries, I have sought to be clear that the mainstream church of the future needs local churches that I have described as small, progressive, and alive. I remain firm in my conviction that while we need to examine a variety of means of delivering the education our pastors need, the mainstream church must never back away from its responsibility to train theologically literate and pastorally skilled ordained clergymen and clergywomen.

I have also attempted to communicate as best I can what I have learned through my experience in two church traditions, Catholic and Protestant—a belief that the bivocational minister can bring a unique perspective to the ministry and because he or she has a career outside of the formal ministry may also bring a unique perspective to members of the congregation she or he serves.

It is my hope that these reflections may in some way contribute to the life and vitality of an ever changing and always reforming church.

Discussion Questions:

1. Comment on the author's specific suggestions for denominational officials and seminaries.

2. State your view regarding the author's specific suggestion for the training of part-time and bivocational ministers. Identify the strengths and weaknesses in the approach he suggests.

3. What is your overall evaluation of the underlying thesis of this book as you understand it?

Appendix A

ESTABLISHING CHURCH GOALS WHEN
CONSIDERING CALLING A PART-TIME PASTOR

This brief questionnaire can be completed by all members of the congregation early in the church's process in constructing a profile for search and call purposes. A congregation should utilize all means possible to acquire feedback through this survey. It can be distributed at church, via mail, and electronically. Procedures for returning it should be established so as to get the most potential input.

1. List the five most important activities done by this church. (Note: This does not necessarily refer to events such as a particular church dinner. It may refer to such activities as preaching, worship, music, and so on.) It may include activities in which the church is not currently involved. If possible, list them in order.

2. What is your expectation of specific activities that the pastor should lead? Please explain briefly.

3. What is your expectation of the amount of time a pastor should spend here at the church over the course of the week? Please explain your answer.

4. (Specifically for churches considering moving from a full-time to a part-time pastor.) What is your opinion of a possible move to a part-time pastor? Please list both the positives and the negatives that you see in this possibility.

5. What do you see as the current strengths and weaknesses of this church?

6. Please indicate what concerns you have, if any, about the future of this church. Is there anything you really fear?

7. Please indicate your gender and age.

8. How long have you been part of this church?

9. As this church moves to calling a new pastor, what do you expect from your own ministry as a member of this congregation? How do you plan to be involved in church life over the next few years?

10. What are your hopes and dreams for this church?

Appendix B

INTERVIEW GUIDELINES FOR SEARCH COMMITTEES

In addition to the interview questions search committees need to ask all prospective pastoral candidates, it is important that they be up front in addressing all issues related to the part-time or bivocational status of a prospective pastor. The significance is even greater when the church has decided to shift away from full-time ministry into a different structure. I strongly encourage committees to take the lead in raising necessary issues. Some areas that need to be addressed:

1. A straightforward explanation of how the congregation views part-time or bivocational ministry. This would include a clear explanation of whether different perspectives exist within the congregation. It also must address this in relation to potential expectations regarding a full-time pastoral model in the church's future.

2. A clear explanation of how the church views specific expectations regarding a pastor's presence and use of time. While I would encourage committees to be flexible and encourage candidates to articulate their vision regarding these issues, it is important that the committee be as up front as possible so as to avoid problems down the road.

3. The questions the committee formulates should be clear and specific. They should encompass (a) the candidate's understanding and expectations of his or her presence on site, and (b) the candidate's sense of priorities in this arrangement.

Following are questions that I would recommend committees use and adapt to specific circumstances:

1. Evaluate yourself as a time manager.

2. Based on your understanding of this congregation, how do you envision the priorities you will set for your time spent among us?

3. Where does serving this church fit into your personal professional goals at this point in your life?

4. (If bivocational) How will working in your other job be a help and a hindrance in the ministry of serving the church as our pastor?

5. What do you see as some differences between full- and part-time ministry?

6. What can a part-time minister do to assure a congregation of the level of his or her dedication to them?

I encourage committees to use these questions as starting points so that they may develop specific inquiries that address their real concerns. Given the complexity of issues potentially involved, it is best to be thorough and transparent in developing questions and in asking follow-up questions that address the real concerns of people in the congregation.

Appendix C

SUGGESTIONS FOR CANDIDATES SEEKING
A PART-TIME OR BIVOCATIONAL POSITION

As stated in the precious appendix, apart from any questions regarding part-time or bivocational status, the candidate should utilize the interview as an opportunity to assess the possibilities inherent in this pastoral opening. In addition, the candidate should be prepared to address specific issues related to the uniqueness of a part-time and/or bivocational arrangement.

Develop a document for presentation to the search committee that explains in specific terms how you approach part-time and bivocational ministry. If you have served in such a capacity before, lay out exactly how it worked. I cannot emphasize enough the importance of specifics.

Ask questions that will help you ascertain the current climate of not only the search committee, but that of the entire church on some relevant issues that must be addressed. My experience has taught me that quite often search committees are ahead of the rest of the congregation in thinking through some of these issues. This makes sense, as they are expected to meet regularly to focus on questions related to the search. It is important that the candidate receive the best possible information about the tone and tenor of the congregation regarding these issues. Not doing so could be harmful in the long run.

Do not assume that the committee will tell you everything you need to know. Trust your own instincts and be willing to address areas in which you know in your gut that you really need more information. It is not good to go into a new call with an uneasy feeling, especially when that can be avoided . . . and it definitely can be, but it's up to you!

Here are some topics that the candidate should be sure are addressed:

1. The different attitudes about part-time or bivocational ministry prevalent in the congregation.

2. Relevant historical facts concerning this issue, including debates and divisions. Some committees (and churches) are more willing than others to admit that dissent might exist.

3. The specific, agreed-upon expectations of the search committee regarding office hours and/or the willingness to have negotiations on this issue.

4. The worst-case scenarios regarding pastoral emergencies, funerals, and the like.

5. The congregation's future expectations—do they plan to move into a full-time arrangement in the future? If so, when?

6. Who else is available to do specific tasks and lead programs important to the church's life? This may include a director of Christian education, youth minister, administrative assistant, pastoral outreach coordinator, or other important personnel.

7. Ask questions based upon your specific review of the documents (for example, the church profile) with which you have been presented.

8. Most importantly, ask anything else that you just sense, way down deep inside, needs to be asked!

The candidate must enter the interview having done a thorough review of the church profile and other relevant documents. It is important that he or she interact with the documentation and formulate questions relevant to how the candidate would see himself or herself in a pastoral position serving this church as it is described. I cannot emphasize enough the importance of thorough preparation for this interview and a willingness on the candidate's part to confront the tough questions that need to be addressed.

Appendix D

A RELEVANT SERMON

Preaching is an integral part of a pastor's work, be he or she full-time, part-time, or bivocational. I include the following sermon, to which I have referred in this book, as an example of many of the ideas we have explored. I hope you will find in this message a vision of a church that is a full-time reality, in spite of the fact that its pastor is employed part-time. I hope that the importance of the "priesthood of all believers" shines through and that you will see in it the significance of executive leadership on the part of the part-time pastor and the ways in which the preached word at the community's worship can help shape and galvanize the local church community to identify and to live out the implications of its shared identity. I hope you get a sense of the real-life church experiences and issues that formed the backdrop for this sermon, and I especially hope that you find it helpful in considering the issues we have discussed in this book. (Note: Capital letters throughout are my visual aid for emphasis while preaching.)

THE MOST DREADED SERMON

This sermon was preached January 25, 2005, at the Congregational Church of Union (Connecticut), United Church of Christ, by the Reverend Robert R. LaRochelle, pastor.

There are few things that turn people off more about church than listening to preachers talk about money. That is a well-documented fact. It makes sense that this would alienate people, if you stop and think about it, because most of us spend a lot of time in the course of our week thinking about money. We go to our mail-boxes, and there sit more bills. January has come, so it's now time to pay for Christmas. Loans, mortgages, investments, mutual funds, nursing home bills, college tuition (that's what they tell me!), home improvement costs, credit cards . . . so many of us live in a financially driven world. Young people worry about whether they will be denied their educational and career dreams, the school they wish to attend, the job they would like to have, all because of MONEY or the lack thereof!

I don't think most of you wake up on Sunday morning, get ready and dressed for church, then get in your car and drive over here, all the while thinking: "I sure hope our pastor talks about money this morning." Do you?? I don't think most people consider joining a church because the minister's a good fund raiser, right? Actually, why DO you come to church? My suspicion is that here you find some kind of refuge from the worries and anxieties of your everyday life. That's what we sang about this morning, didn't we? "Sweet hour of prayer, sweet hour of prayer, that calls me FROM A WORLD OF CARE." There are all kinds of worries and cares OUT THERE! Here in this place, I would suspect, you find welcoming, acceptance, fellowship—whatever very good word you choose to use. There's something different IN HERE from what we are used to OUT THERE. Most of us know that, and so our defenses go up when a church sermon sounds too much like a stewardship campaign kickoff, when the church itself becomes indistinguishable from other human institutions!

Actually, the last time I heard one of those money sermons in church, I just felt like getting up and screaming. The pastor was going on about increased heating and plumbing costs and how consequently the budget had taken a major hit and it would be really good if people would put more in their weekly Sunday offering. All the while, I sat there thinking: "What is he TALKING ABOUT? NOTHING is going on in this church. It is dull and lifeless! He wants people to give so we can have well-heated funerals?" Now, friends, that sounds like a snide, nasty thought and comment, doesn't it? And I will get back to it eventually this morning, hoping to place it in larger context!

Anyway, acknowledging all of the negativity associated with discussing money in church, I have decided to do just that today. I have decided to discuss money and to preach what I have dubbed "The Most Dreaded Sermon." Over the next few minutes, I am going to delve into topics that make many of us churn inside as we sit in our pews. I will talk about MONEY, about GIVING, and about STEWARDSHIP. I have decided to do this on the day of our church's ANNUAL MEETING. An annual meeting, in my mind, is a GREAT church tradition, and I implore you to make every effort to come. I am intentionally preaching this sermon today, the day of our meeting, the day set aside on our calendar to REVIEW our church year and make choices about our future, and I ask a big favor of you this morning: If I preach it in a way that YOU FEEL is unfaithful to the gospel of Jesus Christ, I want to know about it! In fact, you'll get a chance right after church, as members of our Parish Project Group will be asking you to evaluate what you have heard today in this message. So, please, be forthright and honest in your response, as I know you will!

I'm preaching this today because, you see, my friends, here's the situation: Toward the end of 2004, our Budget Committee met several times. In early 2005, they have met again. Later today, you will hear more about their work, but one clear FACT, which has driven many of their discussions, is that there is a definite GAP between what we spend and what we take in each year in offerings and pledges. As I said, that's a simple fact. There's also another dynamic operative here: What we are doing as a church is expanding. You can read my annual report, so I won't repeat it all here, but, you know what I am talking about: Just look at this great handicapped access project as example, or our WELCOMING initiative, reaching out to new Union residents, the fantastic things that are happening with our youth, the kind of musical and worship options we are offering. Actually, our attendance has increased to the point where, according to those who study and analyze church growth, we are now entering into a different CATEGORY when it comes to church size, no longer listed among the really small churches that dot the landscape of our nation. As Jeannine states so succinctly in her excellent report, we are experiencing GROWING PAINS. In a letter I wrote to members of our Budget Committee this past December, here's how I described our situation. I share this with you because I believe it is relevant for ALL OF US:

"In my view, we are at a CROSSROADS period in the life of our church. Due to financial circumstances, we need to ask some important questions. The most important of all is how we envision our church. As pastor, my tendency has been to encourage new programs and outreach. You have been extremely supportive of these efforts and endeavors . . ."

AND THEN I WROTE:

"I raise this issue now because I have thought often of how, one day down the road, this church will be searching for another pastor. In a real sense, part of my responsibility is to bridge the period between now and then as others in the past have most certainly done so well. It is important that, as part of my responsibility, I help us discern the kind of church we want to be, not only today, but IN THE YEARS WHEN WE ARE NO LONGER HERE. As we have sung so often at important times in our church's history, we stand in unbroken line with those who've gone before and with God's saints who one day shall follow."

This morning, my friends, in spite of, maybe BECAUSE OF, these growing pains and our location right here at the CROSS-

ROADS, our church, in my honest view, is really IN A WONDER-
FUL, BLESSED SITUATION! Not wonderful because we happen
to be a few thousand dollars off from a really balanced budget, but
WONDERFUL INSTEAD because circumstances have truly prod-
ded and forced us to look at what it means to BE the Congregational Church of Union, Connecticut, United Church of Christ.
These circumstances might provide us the necessary incentive and
drive to consider what each of us can do individually AND what
we can do COLLECTIVELY, TOGETHER, to be the community
our Lord Jesus is calling us to be.

Most of us prefer to avoid chaotic and uncomfortable circumstances, yet experience so often shows that from them can come
fantastic and serendipitous things. I cite as example this morning.
Sarah needed this Sunday off to go to Virginia to visit Bill's new-
born twin nieces, and Jim was committed to the other Union
Church, the one in Rockville. We had no music! Panic struck deep
in the pastor's heart! "No, they can't endure me playing more than
one song on the organ, God. And this is going on tape to Chicago!"
But look what happened: People came forward and offered to lead,
terrific young members of our congregation and good friends from
the church in Vernon that holds so special a place in my heart.
From this seeming chaos came opportunity and from this opportunity, dear friends, came music and celebration! They stepped forward with a VISION of what it means to worship, with a hope that
by playing some notes on a keyboard or guitar, we'd all be drawn
into something larger and greater than ourselves, drawn, my
friends into the PRESENCE and the WORSHIP of . . . God!

ANY DISCUSSION, my friends, of MONEY and CHURCH
BUDGETS has to start with a vision: Who are we as a church?
Who do we want to be? How do we envision the future? What will
this church be in 2010? In 2015? That's why we are taking time
this Wednesday to gather as a church in prayerful retreat; younger
and older alike, please come. We're not going to talk about money,

I promise. We won't follow up this morning's sermon with THE MOST DREADED RETREAT. Of that can you be sure! But any discussion of what we're going to spend and when we are going to spend it can't be made on the fly. It has to come from a deeper sense of WHO, in fact, WE TRULY ARE!

You see, the whole question of WHERE we spend our money, whether it's in our personal lives or in our life together as a church, is really always a DEEPLY SPIRITUAL QUESTION. A lot of people dismiss real world stuff as NONSPIRITUAL. That's not how the Bible saw it. The Bible is very real-worldly!! In early Genesis, which we heard this morning, and again in the short Deuteronomy passage that followed, we see that this whole notion of giving BACK TO GOD from what God has given us was deeply ingrained in the spiritual psyche (interesting phrase!) of the Jewish people. Obviously, it has become a pretty big part of Christian tradition; otherwise why would ushers come around with offering plates at virtually every service?

GIVING BACK TO GOD FOR WHAT WE HAVE RECEIVED is deeply biblical and clearly SPIRITUAL, BUT . . . and here is where professional church fund-raisers would have my head on a platter: DOES GIVING BACK TO GOD ONLY MEAN GIVING TO THE CHURCH? Let me go back to the example I used earlier. I honestly did NOT think that that particular church I spoke about had been responsive to the needs of youth in the community, nor did I believe that the church offered the community what the community needed. As a result, I really felt that we were spending money for a virtually unused building and that the church was, in reality, a poor steward of the gifts bestowed upon us by God. In my view, in that context, GIVING BACK TO GOD might have meant giving money to the American Cancer Society or to the local homeless shelter or to diabetes research or even to programs for youth in other churches, but to give to THAT church was, in effect, irresponsible stewardship. Now, that's a different take on the issue, isn't it?

Now, please hear this carefully, the very same Bible that espouses giving back to God also places GREAT RESPONSIBILITY on us, the local churches. How about that powerful passage from Acts? "Now the whole group of those who believed were of one heart and soul . . . They laid the property they sold at the apostles' feet and it was distributed to those who had any need." WOW!! The New Testament is clear that the church is called to assume awesome responsibilities, to take care of one another and to reach out to those in need.

I don't want to embarrass you, Hazel, but you all know how Hazel devotes so much time to our children, right? I've got to tell you, though, that one of the greatest things Hazel does for all of us is that she comes into my office on Sunday mornings in March and June and September and she'll remind me: "Could you be sure to mention when you do announcements that we are collecting for our MISSION PROJECT?" Even in the warmest weather, she's reminding the church that there are going to be people cold and shivering come wintertime and that it is our MISSION as church to care for them. She won't let the church run away from those words of Jesus: "When I was hungry, you gave me something to eat. . . . When I was naked, you gave me something to wear!"

It is my sincere belief, my friends, that, unlike that church with which I struggled, ours is a church to which we can feel comfortable contributing. While we are not perfect, we are moving in the right direction, caring for our children and youth, offering aid and assistance to families both in Union and beyond the boundaries of this town. Yet I am also here to say to you this morning that contributing is not only about giving money. Sometimes people just can't. At various times in our lives, we or our children or family members of an older generation may have medical needs that must be met. God would never want us to abandon those people in order to give more money to the church. I had a conversation once with a church member, from a Protestant church here in

Connecticut, who told me that a member of the Stewardship Committee comes to members' homes during pledging season and pretty much tells those folks how much they can afford to give the church. Truth be told, that sickens me. As a pastor, I always worry that we not turn off people who might be interested in coming to church but are worried that they can't live up to a church's financial expectations. That's just not right!

My suggestion is that, in any conversation about stewardship, we need to expand our definition of CONTRIBUTION! Not only do we need to expand it but we also need to celebrate the MANY WAYS people give of themselves as they volunteer to make this church what God wants us to be. Let's applaud those who work with our children, who prepare our worship, who volunteer to sing, who read God's Word to us, who come to Bible study, who keep our property in good shape so that we can house the many worthwhile activities that we do. I'm being literal now, let's applaud them!! (APPLAUSE!) Perhaps some of you sitting here this morning have a talent to share or a gift to offer and haven't had the time or the inclination to do so quite yet. Maybe it would be the gift of a new idea (do you know how many great things happen as a result of new ideas?), perhaps the gift of time. In reality, it's all between you and God, but would you please consider what you CAN do to help make this church what a church ought to be? And, PLEASE, do not underestimate your gift. From what you give, God WILL do great and glorious things! BELIEVE THAT!! PLEASE!

Of course, dear friends, if you can help BRIDGE THAT GAP between income and expenses, if your contribution entails a financial dimension, if that is possible in your life, of course, that would help. I hope this doesn't sound like an infomercial. It's not intended to be. I can't say any of this better than Bob Tyler did in that letter to the congregation we all received and which is reprinted in our recent newsletter. If you get a chance, please go back to that letter. What's written there is really, really good, in my view. If it's within your means to expand your financial giving and if it makes good sense to you in conscience before God, it most certainly would make a big difference. But that's not my decision to make, is it? It's not for me or anyone else to tell you what to give.

But it IS my responsibility, as your pastor, to preach the gospel and to place before us the words of Jesus, the One who told you and me that for those of us who have received much, much also is required! In fidelity to the words of Jesus, we each must make our own decisions. Some might increase our financial giving, others increase the work we do at church. Some might suggest new programs or raise questions about future possibilities. As for me, I am itching to see if there's energy and impetus for us to try a youth musical sometime in the future, a musical that WOULD have the side effect of bringing in a good amount of money, believe me! Still others might realize that, in fidelity and responsible stewardship, we owe our beloved at home much more of our time and attention than we've previously given and, in faithfulness to God, we can't give the time at church we used to give. We'll make personal decisions before our God, all the while mindful that together, in presence and spirit, whether we are in this building or not, we ARE the Congregational Church of Union. These personal decisions we shall make will reflect the kind of church we want to be, not only today, but long into the future, the kind of legacy we'll leave for those who will write histories yet to come.

And so, then, as we go to our annual meeting, where we'll crunch numbers and look at the structures we have in place in this moment of CROSSROADS, this time of healthy and wonderful growing pains, in anticipation of discussions and discernment still to come, I will end this sermon the way I wrapped up that letter to the Budget Committee, with a few editorial variations, looking forward to how God will shape us, in days and months ahead:

In the end there are probably two ways of being the Congregational Church of Union, UCC. In model A, we're a church that's open on Sunday mornings; people know we are here, but we're not going to do a whole lot to get the word out to those people who aren't. We'll want good preaching and worship, but we'll understand that we can never get what those bigger churches get and so we'll be content with who we are. We'll wish we could attract and involve more youth, but we'll understand that youth tend not to like church.

In Model B, however, we will ask a lot of questions. We'll want to know if we can do more to let people know we are here and encourage them to come. We won't give up trying because people we know have been turned off by the churches of either their youth or adulthood. We'll question whether the ways that used to work are going to work any more. And, when we conclude that they won't, we won't bemoan their loss, but rather we'll find new ways. We'll go out into the community, bringing the church to places it has not been. We'll make a major effort to engage our youth in leadership and to encourage them to bring their friends along. We will never accept that because we are small, we can't be very good, and we will make sure that we are! We'll be certain to think about the poor and the needy first and foremost and, though we can't give a lot, we will do the best that we can.

WE WILL UNDERSTAND that to make all of this work, we will have to be CREATIVE, INNOVATIVE, and GIVING—of time and of talent and of money. We'll be exciting and energetic and Spirit-filled and alive. For a small, but GROWING number of people in Connecticut's smallest town, we will refuse to hide our little lamp under a bushel. WE WILL PUT IT OUT THERE FOR EVERYONE TO SEE!

As a proud, though fairly new, member of this church and as your pastor, on this annual meeting day of discussion and decision, even though it's not really on the agenda, I'm going to cast my vote for MODEL B.

May God bless the Congregational Church of Union, Connecticut, United Church of Christ! Amen.

Notes

Introduction

1. This refers to the American Religious Identification Survey done in 2008 by researchers at Trinity College, Hartford, Connecticut.

2. The term "evangelical" in relation to churches shall be used to describe those churches that are generally considered to be more conservative with respect to biblical scholarship and interpretation in relationship to issues of ethics, church leadership, and doctrine. In using this term, I am mindful of the fact that many "mainline" churches are in fact "evangelical" churches as well. This historical fact is often lost in contemporary usage of the term. Nonetheless, I will use it in the popular sense as a way of distinguishing churches. I am also aware that many who claim to be evangelicals and conservative Christians are not "fundamentalists" in the pure sense of that term. I hope these definitions are helpful in terms of using a common language.

Chapter One

1. I refer here to such online resources as www.textweek.com and the like, which provide a wide array of biblical commentary based on lectionary readings.

Chapter Two

1. The term "e word" was used for "evangelism" in a United Church of Christ marketing campaign.

2. Considerable study has been done by organizations such as the Indianapolis Center for Congregations, The Alban Institute, and Hartford Seminary. This information has been widely disseminated.

3. Herman Hupfeld, lyrics and music, "As Time Goes By," from *Casablanca*, © 1931 Warner Bros. Music Corporation, ASCAP.

Chapter Three

1. The United Church of Christ publishes monthly "United Church Employment Opportunities" on its website, which can be accessed directly at http://www.ucc.org/ministers/search-and-call/united-church-employment.html. In recent years there appears to be an increase in bivocational postings.

2. The Presbyterian Church, USA, has published extensive material on its website at http://www.pcusa.org/ministers/models/tentmaking .htm.

3. See Dennis Bickers, *The Tentmaking Pastor* (Grand Rapids: Baker Books, 2000).

4. See Luther Dorr, *The Bivocational Pastor* (Nashville: Broadman Books, 1988).

5. For a thorough historical review of this, see Nathan Hatch, *The Democratization of American Christianity* (New Haven and London: Yale University Press: 1989).

6. See Dennis Bickers, *The Bivocational Pastor* (Kansas City: Beacon Hill Press, 2004).

7. This is drawn from a review of a considerable body of literature about small churches as part of my doctoral thesis: "All Are Welcome: Preaching and the Development of Church Identity in a Small Town," Chicago Theological Seminary: 2007.

Chapter Four

1. This is a paraphrase of one of Luther's sayings regarding the priesthood of all believers. See also 1 Peter 2:9.

2. See Patrick McCaslin and Michael G. Lawler, *Sacrament of Service: A Vision of the Permanent Diaconate Today* (New York/Mahwah, N.J.: Paulist Press, 1986).

Chapter Five

1. See Roy Oswald, "How to Minister Effectively in Family, Pastoral, Program, and Corporate-Sized Churches" in *Action Information*, 17/2 (March/April 1991): 1–7.

2. See Union Historical Society, *Union Lands: A People's History* (Monson, Mass.: Blachley's Printers, 1984).

3. The full text of this hymn may be found in Michael A. Cymbala and Robert J. Batastini, ed., *Gather: Comprehensive* (Chicago: GIA Publications, 1994).

4. This is developed extensively in my aforementioned doctoral thesis.

Chapter Six

1. The Interim Ministry Network (http://www.imnedu.org/education .htm) provides extensive training for this specialized ministry in the church.

2. See *Manual For Ministry* (Cleveland: United Church Press, available at http://www.ucc.org/ministers/manual/).

3. UCC, "Completing the Local Church Profile," available at http://www .ucc.org/ministers/pdfs/local-church-profile-pdf-revised-7-07.pdf.

4. Billy Martin was a well-known baseball manager. In addition to his great success at winning games and championships, he was also noteworthy for the many times he was fired after a limited time on the job!

Chapter Seven

1. See G. Lloyd Rediger, *Clergy Killers* (Louisville: Westminster John Knox, 1997).

2. See Henri Nouwen, *The Wounded Healer* (Garden City: Doubleday Image Books, 1972).

References

Some of the works listed are not cited within the book but are excellent resources for the topics discussed. I have found this material helpful in exploring church demographics and historical trends, small churches, and issues of pastoral ministry in the church, including bivocationality. I hope this list serves as a good starting point for your own exploration:

Bass, Diana Butler. *Christianity for the Rest of Us.* New York: HarperOne, 2006.

Bickers, Dennis. *The Bivocational Pastor.* Kansas City: Beacon Hill Press, 2004.

Bickers, Dennis. *The Tentmaking Pastor.* Grand Rapids: Baker Books, 2000.

Bierly, Steve. *How to Thrive as a Small-Church Pastor.* Grand Rapids: Zondervan, 1998.

Carroll, Jackson, ed. *Small Churches Are Beautiful.* San Francisco: Harper and Row, 1977.

Dorr, Luther. *The Bivocational Pastor.* Nashville: Broadman Press, 1988.

Dorsey, Gary. *Congregation: The Journey Back to Church.* Cleveland: Pilgrim Press, 1998.

Hatch, Nathan. *The Democratization of American Christianity.* New Haven, London: Yale University Press, 1989.

McCaslin, Patrick, and Michael Lawler. *Sacrament of Service.* New York/Mahwah, N.J.: Paulist Press, 1986.

Nouwen, Henri. *The Wounded Healer.* Garden City, N.Y.: Doubleday Image, 1972.

Oswald, Roy. "How to Minister Effectively in Family, Pastoral, Program, and Corporate Sized Churches" in *Action Information* 17/22 (1991).

Oswald, Roy M., and Robert E. Friedrich. *Discerning Your Congregation's Future.* Herndon, Va.: Alban Institute, 1996.

Rediger, G. Lloyd. *Clergy Killers.* Louisville: Westminister John Knox, 1977.

Robinson, Anthony. *Leadership for Vital Congregations.* Cleveland: Pilgrim Press, 2006.

Roof, Wade Clark. *Spiritual Marketplace: Baby Boomers and the Remaking of American Religion.* Princeton and Oxford: Princeton University Press, 1999.